NON-MAMMALS ATTACK!
by Jason Paul Collum

Natural horror films—films with killer animals or plants—exist as far back as 1925 with *The Lost World*. Killer fish, dinosaurs, bugs, reptiles, and flowers have come in all shapes and sizes and for various reasons. Typically, some sort of nuclear radiation (1954's *Them!*), secret science project (1978's *Piranha*), or toxic sauce—*Empire of the Ants* (1977)—is to blame. More recently, there's been a crack in the earth allowing prehistoric creatures to emerge—like *Cloverfield* (2008) or *Piranha 3D* (2010)—or it's been weather gone crazy, like in all six installments of the *Sharknado* franchise. Then, of course, there are the "nature retaliates" plots of films such as *Day of the Animals* (1977), 1976's *The Savage Bees* (and its sequel, *Terror Out of the Sky* [1978]), *Kingdom of the Spiders* (1977), and *The Swarm* (1978). Most frightening of all are the everyday animals who are simply hungry, as in *Open Water* (2003), *Grizzly* (1976), and the mother of these films: *Jaws* (1975). We also can't forget the "whatever versus whatever" films so that we can pit old pop culture figures against each other, like Debbie Gibson versus Tiffany in *Mega Python*

vs. Gatoroid (2011).

Arguably, the goal of most nature-centered horror films is to discover how many humans can be obliterated by the closing credits scroll. Some are highly entertaining, such as *Ticks* (1993), *Arachnophobia* (1989), and any of *The Fly* films, from Vincent Price to Jeff Goldblum. Others sink to depths of ridiculous boredom, such as *Nightwing* (1979), *Tintorera: Killer Shark* (1977), and, yes, *The Food of the Gods* (1976). When reading through film books, retro horror mags, and even current-day mags and online offerings, I'm always struck by how often "nature amok" movies of the 1970s are the focus. Why? My kids (if I had any) are now the main consumers of horror (and I'm heading toward my grandpa years, so even fewer of my age group are spending their time scrolling Amazon Prime's terror lineup). The creature features of the '70s aren't exactly known for their high-end special effects. So, why would my generation remember them, and how could they lure in a 15-year-old to this day? Beyond the camp factor, what makes for the best of nature running amok that keeps each new generation coming back?

The best, most impactful creature feature is dependent on the use of the screenwriter's objective. This is a character study wherein nature simply stands in as a representation of the human emotions and behaviors on display. The natural horror, you see, actually takes a back seat to what's truly being discussed. Think about these classics and cult favorites: After nearly 60 years, people are still watching them repeatedly. Yet, how much do the creatures actually participate in these stories?

Obviously, we begin with the grandmother of them of them all: *The Birds* (1963). Alfred Hitchcock's seminal eye-peckers converge upon a small coastal town and send it into chaos and terror. Townspeople blame outsider Melanie (Tippi Hedren), who has simultaneously just arrived in town and who experiences the first attack. Could it be because she is battling teacher Annie (Suzanne Pleshette) for the heart of stud Mitch (Rod Taylor)? Is it because the birds are the angry voice of mother nature? Or is it possibly Mitch's mother, Lydia (Jessica Tandy), enraged with jealousy at Melanie for "stealing" her son away? The brilliance of screenwriter Evan Hunter's script (based on a sort-of true story by Dame Daphne du Maurier) is that there are so many layers to the story, the cause is likely all of the above. The birds clearly represent the anger, fear, and frustration resulting from the characters' personal issues. Is the title about our fine feathered fiends, or are the birds really the people forced to deal with each other as they are holed up in the cages of their homes (see *Night of the Living*

The Birds come home to roost. (Copyright 1963 Universal Pictures. All Rights Reserved.)

Pasta made incorrectly. (Copyright 1976 The Squirm Company. All Rights Reserved.)

Dead [1968])? *The Birds* gives the viewer neither an answer nor an ending. That's done on purpose. It's the viewer's job to suss it out. (If only 1993's *The Birds II* had made even a minor attempt to be as thought-provoking.)

The direct stepchild of Hitchcock's avian classic, Jeff Lieberman's *Squirm* (1976), claimed to be based on a true story. Much like *The Birds*, the "truth" in the actual events is very minuscule, but the drama seems very real. Minus the classic "worm-face" and over-the-top finale, the events surrounding the disappearing residents of Fly Creek, Ga., seem rather plausible. In an easy role reversal, city boy Mick (Don Scardino) finds himself uncomfortably out of place when he visits his new girlfriend, flame-haired Geri (Patricia Pearcy), much to the chagrin of Roger Grimes (R.A. Dow), who is madly in love with her. Sound familiar? It's a now familiar plot device, but what makes *Squirm* work is that the relationships seem real, even the relationships with the unwelcoming townsfolk (who were real-life citizens of the filming location). These aren't actors "acting," but rather people living their daily, backwoods lives. Yes, worms eat people's flesh clean off their bones, but that suspension of disbelief aside, real bloodworms and bristleworms were used for the majority of the film.

Yet, even though it's those slimy little suckers we've come to see (just like the birds, who would have eaten their pointy asses), writer/director Lieberman has them take a back seat to the struggle between the personalities of their human counterparts. Inferiority complexes come into play between Mick, Roger, and the local yokels. The trick is that it's coming from both sides: Mick feels inferior because he's a city boy and realizes he's guilty of having some preconceived notions of how the locals live. At the same time, the locals feel inferior to Mick because he's a city boy, and they think he's judging them negatively, even though he's not. Numerous legit scares and a healthy dose of suspense have also kept this title alive over 40 years later.

Bullying and isolation factor into *Willard* (1971) and *Ben* (1972), the stories of killer rats that stand up to schoolyard tyrants. *Willard* is the darker of the two films. Its titular character (Bruce Davidson) is a put-upon twentysomething who takes revenge upon everyone who does him wrong by attacking them with his pet rats, Socrates and Ben. While the film is relatively bloodless, shadows and music create an uneasy atmosphere, enhanced by a batshit-crazy "performance" by 1935's *Bride of Frankenstein* icon Elsa Lanchester as Willard's mom. The rats are around mostly as Willard's therapists, expressing his dire outrage and pain at constantly being told he's not worthy. The villains here are not the rats; in a bizarre turn of events, the rats are the heroes. We *want* the mean humans to die—until we realize Willard is beginning to lose control. He goes from hero to villain, which is painful for us to see, much in the way we feel defeated when Carrie White succumbs to her own powers.

It is this same weird sense of emotion that drives *Ben*. What's that you yell? "*Ben* is *not* a horror film"? Well, yes, technically it is; it's just meant for little kids, as its PG rating may suggest. Is it scary? No. Gory? Far from it. Suspenseful? Here and there. It's actually better known for its Golden Globe-wining, Oscar-nominated theme song: "Ben," by Michael Jackson. So, why list a title that's one of the least scary films known to man?

This story of Willard's surviving pet, who is taken in and befriended by sickly little Danny (Lee Montgomery), has garnered a healthy cult following. Some are attracted to its campy death scenes, while others are drawn to the so-sweet-it's-gross friendship between Ben and Danny. Yet, it does that *feelings* thing not commonly experienced in today's horror features. Now, it's about the kills and maybe scaring you. Back in the '70s, however, filmmakers spent more time tugging at your heartstrings. That's why you wanted Laurie Strode to make it to November 1st. You dreaded Carrie's prom queen win in slow motion. Here, young Danny is many of us: a lonely child. A child in single-mother-led home. A child bullied by other kids. He finds an outlet for his frustrations through imagination and creativity. Who among us hasn't turned a four-legged critter into our best friend and emotional support? The strength of *Ben* is that we care. Like its predecessor, *Ben* turns what should be the villains into our heroes, while the human "hero" figures are actually the enemy. It may not make you scream, but it just might bring a bloody tear to your eye and cause your little black heart to cough once or twice.

The exact reverse of the saccharine rat and his boy is possibly the most feared human predator on Earth. *Jaws* (1975) chomped through audiences and created what has since become known as the summer blockbuster. If you haven't seen it, you should probably move on to the next article. Much has been made of it, but the story is really as easy as director Steven Spielberg's pitch: A great white shark eats swimmers off Long Island's coast, the local authorities want it kept hushed so as not to ruin the local economy, and three

The names of the 800 rats that played the titular character of Ben have been lost to iniquity. (Copyright 1972 Bing Crosby Productions. Yes really. All Rights Reserved.)

---

very different men team up to take the shark down. Why do we still love this often-repeated movie? It's been done to death time and time again, sometimes for the better (2003's *Open Water* and 2016's *The Shallows*), sometimes for the outrageous (1998's *Deep Blue Sea*), but more often for the worse, including one of the film's own sequels: the 1987 snooze-fest *Jaws 4: The Revenge*. Plain and simple, *Jaws* is a buddy movie with some of the scariest, most suspenseful moments put to celluloid. It thrives on our most primal fear, not just of dying, but feeling ourselves being eaten. Its effectiveness also prevails because, thank goodness, there's not an ounce of CGI in the *Jaws*. Computer graphics didn't exist in 1975. Yes, there was a robot named Bruce in a few shots, but much of this classic uses footage of real sharks, which makes the film just a little too real for our meat-eating senses.

It was not safe to go back into the water in 1977's *Jaws 2*. One *might* argue that this sequel is the more enjoyable of the franchise. Now, hear me out. The first half of *Jaws* contained a multitude of adrenaline-pumping scenes showing the public under attack, while the second half was mostly three grown dudes arguing and getting drunk while trying to catch the shark. *Jaws 2*, however, sets us up with a cast of characters, mostly teenagers, whom we follow for 116 minutes—and they're all very likable. They're also very realistic. These aren't movie teens. They all could have gone to your high school. They're not trying to prove anything or make any major statements about society. They literally just want to spend the day boating. Sure, there's a shark you know is going to make lunch out of a few of them, but do you really *want* it to? Now, yes, Donna Wilkes screams *a lot* in the final 10 minutes, but if you'd never been on a boat before and you were being circled by a man-eater while floating on what is more or less a tarp in the ocean, wouldn't you? Like its groundbreaking inspiration, *Jaws 2* has much in the way of suspense and a few really solid jolts, and that's really why you enjoy dipping into your swimming pool versus the ocean, isn't it?

Even a pool proves deadly in the most popular of the *Jaws* rip-offs. *Piranha* (1978) knew what it was and what it would be compared to, and so it became a solid wink honoring the granddaddy. Here, a couple of skinny-dipping teens accidentally begin the onslaught of a feeding frenzy when their sex romp results in military-enhanced flesh-eaters being released into a nearby river that leads right to a summer camp and resort. Horror references abound in the Joe Dante-directed film, which, with tongue firmly in cheek, expertly teeters between satire and a genuine scare flick. It's also a love letter to genre fans of the 1950s and '60s, featuring Dick Miller (1959's *A Bucket of Blood*), Barbara Steele (1960's *Black Sunday*), Kevin McCarthy (1956's *Invasion of the Body Snatchers*), Keenan Wynn (multiple *Alfred Hitchcock Presents* episodes), Bradford Dillman (1960's *Crack in the Mirror*), and many others. Yes, we've come to see these creepy little suckers munch a bunch of vacationers, but what we find is a group of mostly really likeable people.[1]

Are you catching on to the theme of "really likeable people" yet? *Not wanting people to die* was a common element of horror prior to the mid-2000s. There are plenty of grue and scares to match the guffaws, but when you can still name characters decades later, the screenwriter (John Sayles) has done the job well. (Not as much can be said for *Piranha II: The Spawning* [1981] or its 1995 remake. However, 2010's *Piranha 3D*—and Jerry O'Connell's penis—does deserve a watch.)

As the 1980s wore on, "nature amok" movies had a few bright frights. *Cujo* (1983), *The Nest* (1987), *Monkey Shines* (1988), and *Arachnophobia* all found their strengths in carrying on the '70s tradition of giving critters the second story as their human leads kept viewers invested by battling their own dramas. Marital strife, love triangles, dependence upon others for the simple needs of life, and, yes, sometimes just a group of fun people we enjoy watching, help us meet that need for suspension of disbelief. Yes, *Jaws* can happen. *Squirm* and *The Birds* sort-of happened. Yet, if we're only coming to see awful people die, those special effects had better be able to stand the progression of time (hello, 1989's *Gnaw: Food of the Gods II*). Otherwise, audiences won't keep coming back for more. For every *Cloverfield* (2008), there's a *Mosquito* (1994), *Bats* (1999), or *Mega Scorpions* (2003)…oh, wait, I think I was in that one….

Exploitation Nation Choose-Your-Own-Adventure:

> If you wish to continue with Jason's adventures with attacking animals, **turn to page 48.**

> If you wish to read more about animals attacking from others besides Jason, **turn to page 11.**

---

[1] SPOILER ALERT: Who isn't traumatized when camp counselor Betsy (Belinda Balaski) is pulled down into the murky depths? SPOILER OVER.

DAY OF THE ANIMALS (1977)
by Douglas Waltz

Directed by William Girdler (who gave us *Grizzly* and the totally bizarre *The Manitou* before dying in a helicopter crash) and written by William W. Norton, Eleanor E. Norton, and Edward L. Montoro, *Day of the Animals* begins with factual information concerning the depletion of our ozone layer and the effects that depletion could have on the planet. Jump ahead three years and we get a movie that uses that information to give us another "nature gone amok" film.

But here's where it gets interesting. See, most of the "nature gone amok" films deal with a specific species. *Jaws* had a shark, *Willard* had rats, *Grizzly* had a bear (you get the idea). Each of the traditional "nature gone amok" films deals with a specific species.

Day of the Animals turns that idea up to 11 by having the ozone create a mutated virus that affects animals above elevations of 5,000 feet. In other words, every animal is affected—bears, mountain lions, snakes, spiders, birds, dogs. If one animal gone amok is a box office win, all of them together should be gold, right? Well, kind of.

A hiking group led by Steve Buckner (Christopher George [*Grizzly*, *Pieces*]) is going to be dropped off at the top of the mountain and hike back. Buckner is going to teach them how to live off the land, with no weapons. Sounds fun, right? Ranger Tucker (Walter Barnes [*High Plains Drifter*, *Pigs*]) warns Steve that it might not be a good idea. Things have been strange up on the mountain.

There's the news lady, Terry

Marsh (Lynda Day George [*Pieces, Mortuary*]), out for a vacation away from the big city. We get the single mom, Shirley Goodwin (Ruth Roman [*Go Ask Alice, The Baby*]), and her kid, John (Bobby Porter [*Under the Rainbow, The Nude Bomb*]). There is the married couple trying to get their act together, Frank (Jon Cedar [*The Manitou, Capricorn One*]) and Mandy (Susan Backlinie [*Jaws, The Great Muppet Caper*]). There's also the younger couple, Bob (Andrew Stevens [*The Fury, The Terror Within*]) and Beth (Kathleen Bracken [*The Man with Bogart's Face, Underground Aces*]). Professor MacGregor (Richard Jaeckel [*The Dirty Dozen, The Green Slime*]) is there to take pictures of birds. Daniel Santee (Michael Ansara [*The Manitou, It's Alive*]) is a Native American who used to ignore his heritage but now embraces it. Roy (Paul Mantee [*The Manitou, Robinson Crusoe on Mars*]) is an ex-football player with a career cut short by bone cancer, and Paul Jenson (Leslie Nielsen [*Creepshow, Airplane!*]) is straight from Madison Avenue on a trip just to get away from the city.

On the mountain, it doesn't take long before things get weird. At their first stop they are surrounded by big birds that aren't at all afraid of them. the behavior They discover an abandoned campsite, decide it's as good a place as any. Paul falls asleep when it's his turn to stand watch, and Mandy is attacked by a wolf. The next day, the group gives the food they have to Frank and Mandy and give them directions to the nearby ranger station, the rest continue their hike back down the mountain. ,Isolated, Mandy is attacked by vultures and thrown off the mountain. Frank staggers to a creek, sees a little girl (Michelle Stacy [*Airplane!, Demon Seed*]), and takes her with him.

The next night, the main group is attacked by mountain lions, which leads the group to split in two. Paul is obviously feeling the effects of the aggression virus and leads Shirley, Shirley's son, Bob, and Beth to the ranger station because it's closer.

Steve and his group find an abandoned mine to hole up in just before a downpour. Bob has had enough of Paul, so they fight. Paul decides Beth belongs to him now. A word of warning to people who have fond memories of Leslie Nielsen in his

Uncredited cougar from Day of the Animals.
(Copyright Multicom Entertainment Group Inc. All Rights Reserved.)

comedic roles: at this point in the film, he snaps and gets super rapey. Maybe fast forward until you see a bear.

Yeah, so, a bear arrives. Paul sees that as a challenge and attacks the bear. Yeah, you read that right: He attacks the bear. It doesn't go well for Paul. A fun game to play during this scene is to see how many times you can spot the shitty bear suit. It's a lot.

Suffice to say, the animals have their day. They a crashed around grouphsthe dogs is soon the of them,,Professor MacGregor,,what's left of the groups,. Hbecomes,The next day, the virus has dissipated, the ozone layer has shifted, and everything that was affected has died. Some people made it, some didn't.

George brings his gruff game a year after *Grizzly* and is perfect in the role. (I always thought they put his wife in the movies because he was in the movies.) Ansara does his best "wise Native American," bit even though we all know he's Syrian.

I felt that the movie worked well. The presence of so many trained animals in the days before CGI made this a weird film. If you know anything about nature, it's strange to see birds that don't belong together. Mountain lions don't hunt in packs, but they do in this flick. Thirty-three years later, I distinctly remembered Nielsen impaling Stevens and fighting a bear. Being much younger then, I didn't spot the fake bear suit and the fact that the guy wrestling the bear was in better shape than Nielsen. The film also has a great shot of one of the dogs jumping through a cabin window. For some reason, that decided to stick in my brain all these years later too.

Sometimes, taking a popular-at-the-time film sub-genre (like nature gone amok) and throwing as much stuff as possible at the screen to see what sticks is a really, really bad idea. Other times, it's *Day of the Animals*.

Final thought: After this film, Nielsen would go on to do *Airplane!* and jumpstart a new career for himself. *Airplane!* has the scene with the little boy and girl having coffee. You know the one. Yeah, she's the same little girl from this movie.

13

PIGS 'N CROCS

by Mike Haushalter

When it was revealed that one of the themes of this issue would be "nature attacks," I soon realized just how many I'd seen over my years. Here are just a few of the ones I revisited recently:

Razorback (1984): A ferocious, supersized, bulletproof wild boar is stalking the Australian Outback, and man is its prey. After it claims an American TV journalist as a meal, her grieving husband shows up to find out what became of his wife.

Jaws made huge bank when it hit theaters in 1975. In no time, filmmakers all over the world were trying to get their hands on some of that gold. *Grizzly* came first in 1976, with *Orca* (1977) and *Piranha* (1978) hot on its heels, not to mention shameless *Jaws* rip-offs, such as *Tintorera: Killer Shark* (1977). Nowadays, there are almost too many *Jaws* clones to count, but in 1984, Australia had its go at the sub-genre with the blood-soaked boar-gone-wild thriller *Razorback*.

Razorback is the first feature film from Russell Mulcahy (*Highlander*), the man who pretty much gave birth to MTV. The film is an Ozploitation

Jaws set in the Outback and based on the novel of the same name by Peter Brennan (the creator of TV series *A Current Affair* and *Judge Judy*). As expected, coming from the director of the first music video to play on MTV, *Razorback* is a virtual visual tour de force of wild-hog terror. Sudden zooms, bold lighting and colors, strange camera angles, real animal violence, and more are thrown at the viewer. Almost every scene is milked for maximum visual and aural overload, as to be expected from the man who found fame by directing Duran Duran music videos (the video for "Hungry Like the Wolf" pretty much got Mulcahy the gig).

Something about the locations and sensory overload of *Razorback* really reminds me a good deal of Richard Stanley's films *Hardware* and *Dust Devil*, save that *Razorback* seems to lack any of the subtext or deeper meaning of Stanley's films and, of course, was made a good deal before those films. Unfortunately, *Razorback* is one of the ultimate examples of "all style and no substance." It's just an old-fashioned monster movie pretentiously disguised as an art film. The plot, which is full of horrible characters doing horrible things, is a mess that can't even produce a hero till midway through the movie, and even then, he's kind of a dick. To be honest, a VHS collection of Mulcahy's Duran Duran music videos would have more subtext and coherent storytelling.

In the end, I suppose how much you enjoy *Razorback* just depends on what kind of film you're looking for. As a thrill ride, *Razorback* is as exciting as a county fair Scrambler ride during a firework display—fast, loud, and full of colorful flashes of brilliance. If you want more than an audio/video assault on your senses, you may want to look elsewhere.

Chaw (2009): *Chaw* is a dark, black South Korean horror-comedy about Officer Kim (Tae-woong Eom), a young police officer transferred from South Korea's largest metropolis, Seoul, to a small backwater village in the countryside (after putting "anywhere" as a lark for his second choice on his transfer form). It soon turns out that this seemingly idyllic, crime-free hamlet is under siege by a raging boar.

Chaw is not so much a man-versus-nature film as a nature-versus-man film. It opens with a short, brutal montage of sometimes real animal cruelty and over-hunting that made even a meat-eater like me root for the beast from the get-go.

Despite its grim opening, the first half of the film is more a goofy comedy with brief moments of gore than a taut, tension-building horror-fest the likes of *Jaws*, *Grizzly*, and even the offbeat *Razorback*. It does offer up the typical killed-the-wrong-animal scene and shutdown-the-"beach" scene, though, in this case, the tourists are there to pick organic produce, and the farm owners don't want them scared off just because a wild animal may have killed a few folks.

The second half turns up the

heat with the arrival of a well-armed hunting party and some reward-seeking locals trying to put the boar down (which they do in short order, only, as you may have guessed, it's not the real boar). Not to worry, though, as the beast gets its big reveal at the village pig roast. For what it's worth, there's a pretty good bit of carnage, and the beast looks pretty feisty.

From here on out, *Chaw* sputters to its climax following a ragtag band of misfits taking to the hills to finally slay the beast.

This film is far more quirky than it is scary (What's with the crazy lady who looks straight out of *Ringu* or *The Grudge*?), and its cast all seem like they are taking part in a *Twin Peaks* reenactment instead of a *Jaws* knockoff. Another of its other failings is that every time the film even starts to get exciting, it switches back into low gear and slows things down. Finally, the film also goes on much longer than it should and would have benefited from some tighter editing.

While it was not the thriller I was hoping for, *Chaw* has fairly good monster effects and is a decent *Jaws* knockoff/pastiche that may well be worth a viewing by both fans of horror and Korean cinema.

Boar (2017): A pig of unusual size and ferocity is killing anyone who dares enter the land it has claimed. This results in a night of terror for a family that strays into the bloodthirsty boar's territory while vacationing in the Outback.

Boar was my third killer-pig-on-a-rampage film in just about as many days. It is a swift-moving Australian creature feature directed by Chris

Sun (*Charlie's Farm*). Because the film comes from Australia and is about a boar gone wild, *Razorback* was very much in my mind as I viewed *Boar*, but as it turns out, the two films have very little in common aside from their location and boar antagonists. In reality, *Boar* probably has more in common with the *Friday the 13th* films in that there are several monster-POV shots, the antagonist has ninja-like stealth, and some teens are slayed in their tent before they can do the deed. Also, like Jason, this beastly boar is simply a monster killing-machine, with no cares for self-preservation or any semblance of being a real pig (albeit a huge freaking pig).

Fans of monster carnage should be pleased with the film's many bloody kills and the title beast, which is brought to life through a good mix of CGI and practical effects. The film also boasts a pretty good cast, headlined by Nathan Jones (*Mad Max: Fury Road*), Bill Moseley (*The Texas Chainsaw Massacre 2*), Roger

Ward (*Mad Max*), and John Jarratt (*Wolf Creek*). Ex-powerlifter and World Wrestling All-Stars champion Nathan Jones stands out in particular as the film's hero, Bernie. It turns out that Jones has much more acting ability and charisma than the meat-wall henchmen roles he normally gets (see *The Protector* and *Conan the Barbarian*) would lead you to believe. Moseley also has a good part as the head of the vacationing family, delivering a performance that is much more down-to-earth and real-to-life than most of his genre material.

On the other hand, the film does have a number of flaws. First off, it's got a wafer-thin storyline with an uneven tone. Characters are introduced only to disappear for long stretches of time. The editing is wonky in many places, and the film has a very out-of-place Hollywood happy ending.

Boar is not the best killer pig film I have ever seen, but as monster films go, it's worth checking out.

Pig Hunt (2008): A weekend wilderness retreat to do some pig hunting on the land of his recently departed uncle goes very wrong for John and his friends when they discover the truth behind the legendary 3,000-pound hog nicknamed "the Ripper." Soon, what could have been a relaxing getaway from life in the big city spirals out of control and descends into a grueling battle for survival against both man and beast.

To me, it's a no-brainer that when you mix a group of pig hunting, city slicker dude-bros with tribal, pot farming hippies; backwoods, hillbilly rednecks; and a 3,000-pound boar, things are going to go very, very wrong. *Pig Hunt* was my last of four pigs-gone-wild films, and because it was, I thought I pretty much knew exactly where the pig hunt was going to lead. But by the time the end credits finally rolled, I found my expectations had been skewered like a pig on a spit. This is not just another "nature gone amok," *Jaws/Grizzly* clone. Instead, it is a dark, quirky tale of a hunting trip gone horribly wrong in the same vein as rural horror films such as *Deliverance*, *Southern Comfort*, and *Rituals*, but with the value-added threat of a giant killer hog that is pretty much just teased in the shadows until the big reveal during the third act's blood-soaked climax.

Pig Hunt is a very entertaining, if perhaps overly ambitious, low-budget horror film from director Jim Isaac (*Jason X*), who seems to have had a lot on his mind during filming and wanted to fit it all into the movie. As this was Isaac's last film before his death, maybe it's just as well that he used up all his ideas. He delivered a slow-burn film that has great visual flair and imagination and looks like a big-budget production. It's also a film that is more about character dynamics, rites of passage, and man's inhumanity rather than just another "nature run amok" creature feature. It's a gritty, pedal-to-the-floor throwback to the subversive social-conscience cinema of the '70s that wanted you to think about *and* feel the horrors that unspooled before you. To help accomplish this, the film dishes out plenty of on-screen blood, guts, and T&A thrills, topped off with a lot of close-to-the-surface subtext about gun culture, machismo, racism, and war in the Middle East. All of this results in a very busy potboiler that you will either enjoy for its genres-in-a-blender audacity to be different or lose interest in due to its constant changes in tone and direction.

Lake Placid 3 (2010): Zoologist Nathan Bickerman (Colin Ferguson) and his family move into his deceased aunt's cabin on Black Lake as they ready the house to be sold on the market. Nathan's lonely and friendless son soon takes up where his great-aunt Delores Bickerman (the croc feeder that Betty White played in *Lake Placid*) left off and feeds the resident baby crocodiles. He thinks they are his newfound pets until they grow up to become monstrous alpha predators and begin a terrifying feeding frenzy. Will anyone be able to stop these cold-blooded killers before they devour half the town?

Just when you thought it was safe to turn on your television, the Syfy channel unleashed *Lake Placid 3* in 2010 as one of its late-summer, movie-of-the-week premieres. Two months later, the film was released on DVD as an unrated edition featuring value-added nudity and perhaps a bit more gore. Before *Sharknado* went viral, the Syfy channel made some pretty fun movies-of-the-week, most of which were modest B-movies trying hard to entertain instead of be overblown, Twitter bait "event" films. *Lake Placid 3* was one of them. The film is a fairly entertaining creature feature, complete with a high body count, generous dollop of T&A, and sharp sense of humor. It's got a decent script, was helmed by a mostly competent director (Griff Furst, who directed *Arachnoquake* and starred in a movie written by *EN*'s own Mike Watt, *Dead Men Walking*) and features a good cast—a surprisingly good cast, including Michael Ironside (*Scanners*) as the sheriff; Yancy Butler (*Hard Target*) as Reba, a foul-mouthed, badass poacher (who returns for the next two *Lake Placid* installments); Colin Ferguson (*Eureka*) as the film's bland hero, Nathan; Kirsty Mitchell as his wife, Susan; and Jordan Grehs as their seemingly unwanted son, Conner. With ample eye-candy supplied by Angelica Penn, Kacey Clarke (*Resident Evil: Afterlife*), and fan favorite Roxanne Carrion (*Emmerdale*) as a skinny-dipping hiker whose au naturel demise by a clutch of crocs is well worth the price of a film rental alone. As for the rest of the cast, well, they are pretty much just croc bait and not worth much mention.

The CGI-created monster crocodiles are a bit of a letdown, to

DON'T FORGET YOU'RE LUNCH!

be sure. OK, they pretty much suck, but I have seen worse. At this point, it's also hard to say whether or not the effects would have looked better a decade ago when the film came out. Whatever the case, the filmmakers seemed happy with the CGI work, because they don't try to hide the monsters at any point. The crocs are on-screen quite a lot, racking up almost a dozen bloody kills in plain sight, including one yappy pooch and one brutal decapitation.

All in all, *Lake Placid 3* is a run-of-the-mill monster movie, which most people will assume from the title alone, but if you enjoyed the other *Lake Placid* sequels, you probably will like this one too.

Lake Placid: The Final Chapter (2012): Tenacious, trash-talking poacher Reba (Yancy Butler from *Lake Placid 3*) returns to Black Lake, which, thanks to some tree-hugging conservationists, has now been turned into a crocodile sanctuary. The Army Corp of Engineers has surrounded the lake with an electric fence, and the EPA has put Reba in charge of patrolling the waters (as part of a community service plea bargain, no doubt). When a high-school field trip unknowingly enters the preserve after the fence gate gets left open by a team of poachers, it's up to Reba and sheriff Theresa Giove (Elisabeth Röhm) to save the sheriff's daughter, Chloe, and her fellow students before they all become crocodile bait.

The fourth *Lake Placid* outing is really just not as fun as the last one, which is a shame because it has a lot going for it on the surface. Like the third installment, this film has a good cast of veteran actors, starting with Butler returning as the feisty, foul-mouthed poacher-turned-gamekeeper. She is backed up by Röhm as the lake's newest take-charge sheriff. The film also stars Poppy Lee Friar as Chloe; hunky U.K. star Paul Nicholls as Loflin, the sheriff's Army boy toy; Benedict Smith as Loflin's less-than-likely son, Max (They really should be brothers); and, of course, Robert Englund as a grizzled (What else?), lost Bickerman cousin (Yes, Betty White's Delores Bickerman character from *Lake Placid* has yet another crazy relative). It also has slightly better CGI crocodiles than the last two films, as well as a surprising amount of decent practical effects and props. There are about 14 on-screen deaths, including a few nice dismemberments and a very bloody piranha-themed youngling attack. The film was also shot at a far nicer body of water than the dirty pond location that filled in for a lake in *Lake Placid 3*.

On the minus side, this is a pretty turgid ride that crawls to a start and is not much better once it gets going. It's just a stale film filled with characters who are really hard to believe or care about, save for maybe Chloe, and that's really stretching the definition of the word *care*. At least Chloe feels a bit more like a human than anyone else. Butler gets some juicy dialogue and does what she can, but it's obvious that most of these folks just don't have anything to work with and are going through the motions for a paycheck. This stuff is tedious drivel, even by Syfy standards. It's so bad that, at one point, Butler seems to tell another actress to shape up and do her job rather than her character.

I hate to say this, but when I saw that Butler was making a return appearance and would be joined by Englund, it kind of sounded like a surefire hit to me. So, I was pretty let down by time the last body bit the dirt and the credits rolled.

Lake Placid vs. Anaconda (2015): After surviving a deadly crocodile attack in *Lake Placid: The Final Chapter*, Jim Bickerman (Robert Englund) returns to Black Lake for some payback and ends up setting off a battle between mutated crocodiles and genetically engineered anacondas. It's up to Reba (Yancy Butler), now the new Black Lake sheriff, and Clear Lake game commissioner Will "Tull" Tully (Corin Nemec) to find a way to slay these warring monsters before they destroy the whole town.

By this point, you're probably thinking, "*Lake Placid vs. Anaconda?* Wasn't the fourth *Lake Placid 'The Final Chapter'*?" Did they really make five *Lake Placid* movies (or six at this point, but who's counting…)? You also may be wondering if this can really be a crossover with the *Anaconda* franchise and how exactly either were still relevant by 2015. Yes, the film is a crossover of the two franchises, and oddly enough, it's the fifth film in both series.

This is the first of the *Lake Placid* films to have been made by the Syfy channel after the event that was *Sharknado*, and it shows. The film is loaded with just about everything you can think of: giant snakes; giant crocodiles with ninja skills; evil, multimillion-dollar chemical corporations with secret agendas; salty, hook-handed, peg-legged poachers; and, of course, some local sorority sisters celebrating rush week on the beach.

Like the previous *Lake Placid* offerings, this one has its share of problems. The premise is very hard to swallow, even for a Syfy movie of the

week. It has terrible CGI that, at best, could be described as adequate, not counting the CGI anacondas, which are closer to feeble. The anaconda menace is underused, many of the victims disappear without anyone noticing—and how exactly do 12- to 30-foot crocodiles sneak up on people or, better still, creep under a bed inside a house?

But like its siblings, this *Lake Placid* does have a good cast (Syfy really seems to understand that competent casts go a long way), highlighted by Corin Nemec (*Parker Lewis Can't Lose*) as Tull, the film's heroic game warden. Yancy Butler's Reba, now the new sheriff (This community really goes through sheriffs), returns as well, and Robert Englund is back from the dead as Jim Bickerman, minus a few limbs and an eye (His peg leg may be the film's best effect).

The film also has a wicked sense of humor, fast pacing, and plenty of on-screen mayhem. Also, like *Lake Placid 3*, the unrated version really lives up to its too-hot-for-TV moniker, offering up a ton of topless fan service.

With a title like *Lake Placid vs. Anaconda*, you pretty much know from the get-go if this is the movie for you. I've got to say, I was kind of looking forward to watching it when I found out it was a thing. Was I disappointed? Yes, a little, but it was better than part four, and I would probably watch it again if I had no other options available.

Anaconda 3: Offspring (2008): Let's leave off with a giant snake film. Dr. Amanda Hayes (Crystal Allen), a brilliant herpetologist working in a millionaire's secret lab facility, performs cancer research experiments on two giant mutant anacondas. But when the corrupt industrialist and financier, Murdoch (John Rhys-Davies), pushes the experiments too far, the snakes escape and go on a hungry rampage. A band of mercs are called in to hunt down the mega snakes before they reach a nearby town.

So, I was not really planning on reviewing any films from the *Anaconda* franchise (or even watching any for that matter), but after doing a bit of research for my review of *Lake Placid vs. Anaconda*, I found out that *Anaconda 3: Offspring* starred both John Rhys-Davies and David Hasselhoff, and suddenly I had a reason to watch an *Anaconda* film.

My first thought when I put it in was why in the world was Rhys-Davies headlining a Syfy movie of the week? What in the hell did he do with all that sweet *Lord of the Rings* money? Does he have that many ex-wives? Is he a gambling addict? Anyhow, it's a mystery to me why he turns up in this film (and the next one), but at least he no longer looks like a bag that used to contain Sean Connery like he did when he made *Chupacabra Terror* a few years prior. Hasselhoff, on the other hand, I expect to find in this sort of swill. In fact, I am kind of sad he didn't do more. He always comes off as a douche, but he is a charming douche, and I thought he made a great Nick Fury back in 1998's *Nick Fury: Agent of S.H.I.E.L.D.*

As stories go, *Anaconda 3* is a very by-the-numbers "dangerous science experiment escapes" creature feature that is pretty rote (and I may have seen it before in a dinosaur or shark film), save for some decent jump scares and few moments of humor. You know the drill: lots of running, explosions, and thinly sketched-out characters getting chomped, topped off with a heroic slow-walk from the giant explosion climax.

The CGI effects are as bad as you'd expect but gorier than both the previous *Anaconda* films, and every once in a while, the snakes even look good. There is even a decent amount of bloody practical effects. The filmmakers were certainly pleased with the effects, because just about all the kills are replayed in a flashback sequence in which the heroine reflects on the horror she helped unleash.

As I've said in many of my *Lake Placid* reviews, with a film of this ilk, you pretty much know what you're in for before you press play. Despite all of my faint praise, it's an oddly watchable film that sets up its premise and then just pours on the speed. Of course, since you can also choose to watch *Boa*, *Copperhead*, *King Cobra*, *Mega Snake*, *Python*, *Vipers*, or *Boa vs. Python*, maybe "watchable" just won't pass the muster for some of you.

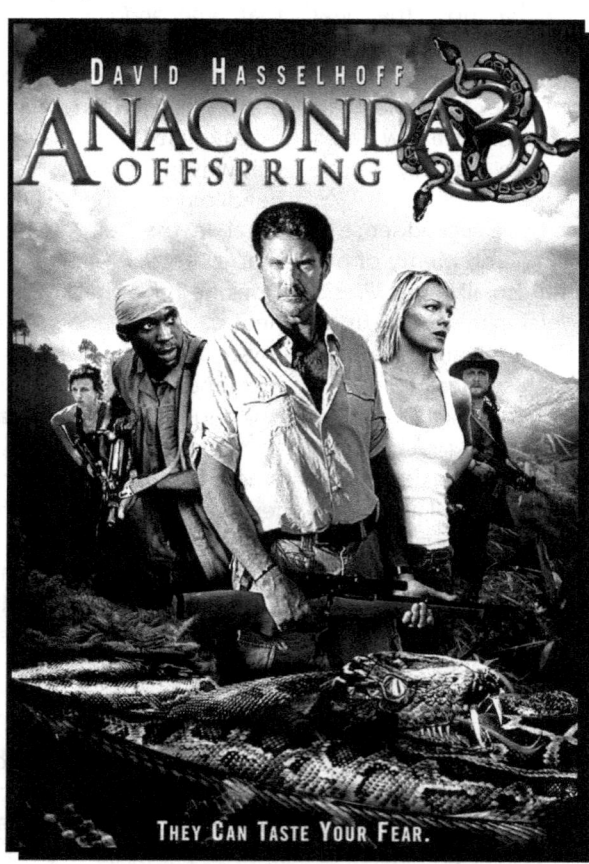

Here. Have some Hasselhoff.

GRAPHIC WORM HORROR!
by Justin Wingenfeld

In 2019, Netflix produced a horror film called *The Perfection*. It is a tale of obsession, jealousy, and revenge involving a rivalry between two female concert cellists (Allison Williams and Logan Browning) and their demanding teacher (Steven Weber), who seems to have more than just their musical career in his mind. It's an interesting film with some decent twists, and it leads up to a dark and gruesome finale.

However, it was not the film's ending that caused unsuspecting viewers to become physically sick. In a scene that repulsed some people enough to turn the film off, Browning gets violently ill while riding a bus and suffers vomiting and diarrhea. As bad as that is, her vomit is writhing with maggots. Even worse, she appears to have insects crawling under her skin. Eventually, the skin of her arm bursts open and dozens of beetles come crawling out. She vomits more bugs and then decides the best course of action is to chop off her hand with a meat cleaver, conveniently provided to her by Williams.

You just don't see that sort of thing in a Netflix movie very often.

To most people, the concept of having worms or insects crawling under their skin or in their internal

The Perfection gets under your skin. (Boo! Bad joke!)
(Copyright Miramax/Capstone Film Group. All Rights Reserved)

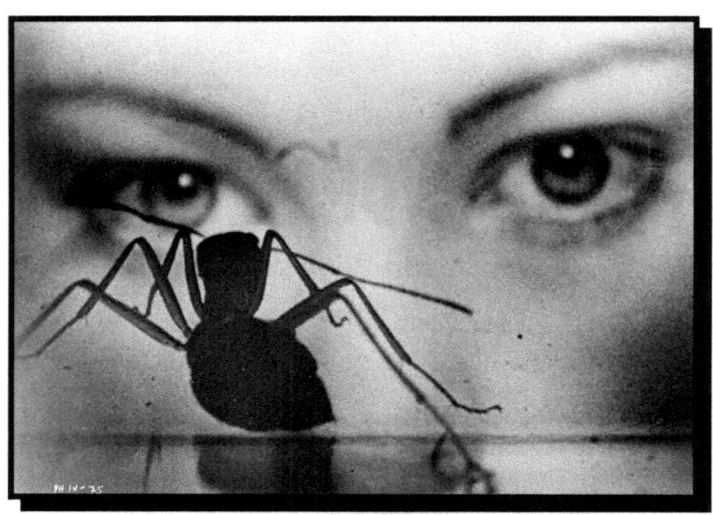

The ants watch us in Phase IV. (Copyright Paramount Pictures. All Rights Reserved.)

---

organs is a particularly unsettling one. The primal aversion to disease and decay causes us to get queasy at the idea of touching a maggot-ridden garbage can lest even one of those squirming little horrors actually manages to crawl onto our hand. If the idea of having them on us is that bad, the idea of having them *in* us must be horrific beyond our wildest nightmares. Yet the idea has seldom been used in horror.

For decades, filmmakers have tried to scare audiences with movies about bugs, be they giant monsters created by atomic radiation or swarms of standard-sized insects, spiders, or worms. Many an arachnophobe would sooner face a charging lion than walk through a spiderweb, and having to make it through a tunnel carpeted with thousands of insects to save Indiana Jones might be a fate worse than death for some.

Be they the super-intelligent ants in *Phase IV* (1974), the pyrokinetic cockroaches in *Bug* (1975), or the mutant worms of *Squirm* (1976), they are at least outside our bodies, allowing for potential escape. But how does one get away from something that's inside one's own body?

The phenomenon of delusional *parasitosis* has, on occasion, been used in film. A mental illness that manifests itself as the belief that one's body and/or surroundings are infested with insects (or some other tiny marauding things), the concept has been used to nauseating effect in the aforementioned *The Perfection*, as well as *Hellbound: Hellraiser II*, for example. It is also the focus of William Friedkin's 2006 thriller *Bug* (no relation to the 1976 William Castle film).

On the other hand, Craig T. Nelson vomits up a demonic monster after drinking tainted tequila in *Poltergeist II: The Other Side* (1985). People are turned into zombies by swallowing parasitic mutant slugs in David Cronenberg's *They Came from Within*

(1975), Fred Dekker's *Night of the Creeps* (1986), and James Gunn's *Slither* (2006), while others are eaten from the inside out by a blob-like organism that just happens to taste great and have zero calories in Larry Cohen's *The Stuff* (1985). Of course, there is no more famous Hollywood parasite than the larval form of the xenomorph, which first burst out of John Hurt and into horror history in Ridley Scott's *Alien* (1979) and reappeared in several sequels, spin-offs, and parodies ("Hello, my baby! Hello, my honey!").

When the infestation is not the result of psychosis, aliens, or malevolent maguey worms, the victim of wriggling, crawling things is more often than not on the receiving end of a spell or curse. Conal Cochran's evil plan in *Halloween III: Season of the Witch* (1982) is to entice kids to don their Silver Shamrock masks during a post-trick-or-treat TV special, at which point an ancient Celtic power (courtesy of Stonehenge) will cause the kids to barf up crickets and rattlesnakes. An impractical way to protest the commercialization of Samhain, but effective nonetheless.

In John Schlesinger's underrated *The Believers* (1987), a police officer investigating a series of ritualistic child murders fatally stabs himself after experiencing horrible abdominal pain. Before doing so, he yells (in Spanish) "Snakes!" Later, his autopsy reveals several of them slithering in his intestines, having been manifested there via Brujería, a voodoo-like Caribbean form of black magic.

Even *Harry Potter and the Chamber of Secrets* (2002) has an admirably disgusting scene in which Ron's attempt to cast a spell on another student backfires, causing him to belch out slugs until the spell wears off.

But the use of creepy crawlers as a means to cause slow, painful death from the inside had its origins in the Hong Kong offices of Shaw Brothers Studio, producers of everything from period melodrama to martial arts action since the 1950s. In the mid-'70s, the Shaws decided to try their hands at a more visceral type of horror film rather than the classy supernatural and ghostly tales that had made up their previous dips into the genre. Gore and sleaze were making American and European film distributors mountains of cash in the early '70s, so the Shaws followed suit, unleashing the appropriately titled *Black Magic* in 1975.

Basically a feature length soap

opera punctuated by scenes of gore, *Black Magic* set a template for a string of similar films, each one more ghoulish than the last. All the staples were established: the outcast sorcerer, bizarre ingredients needed for his concoction, worms and maggots crawling under a victim's skin, and a showdown between evil and benevolent magicians.

Before speed dating was a thing, sometimes all one could do to score was to hire a sorcerer to whip up a love potion. And so it is for the characters of *Black Magic*, who repeatedly secure the services of a freelance practitioner of the dark arts to make the objects of their desire fall for them.

But things get so complicated when *everyone* starts doing it, including the sorcerer himself. Then, a magician who practices white magic has to step in, and really, who needs that headache?

Potions with ingredients such as breast milk, human hair and teeth, maggot-infested flesh, corpse putrescence, and snake blood (yummy!) are the evil sorcerer's bread and butter and are so revolting, complex, and time-consuming that one wonders why his customers don't just try getting their targets drunk. And is it really necessary to inflict their significant others with maggots and worms burrowing under their flesh? Why add insult to injury?

Apparently there was enough lovesick desperation going around to lead to an epidemic, as *Black Magic 2* (1976) deals with medical experts investigating an illness that causes worms to appear under victims' skin and welts (resembling human faces) to appear on their bodies. Medical experts struggle to explain this odd ailment, while the evil magician responsible has moved on to creating a race a zombies to do his bidding, inflicting his enemies with worms and other creepy-crawlies under their skin.

The strange and disgusting Chinese horror plot device of having worms infest a targeted victim possibly originated with the Chinese myth of gu, a potent poison created by having multiple venomous creatures battle each other until only one remained, having consumed the others. The victor was then fed to maggots, which, in turn, proceeded to eat each other, concentrating the venom further and further. The resulting poison was used in rituals to cause everything from sexual attraction to bad luck, illness, or death for an intended victim. While worms and insects appearing in a victim's body was intended to control or harm the victim and only existed in a metaphorical (or metaphysical) way, horror screenwriters soon realized the gross-out potential of worms erupting from skin or being vomited like the green bile that comes spewing from Regan's mouth in *The Exorcist* (a big hit in Asia).

Other Shaw Brothers horror films feature moments of people vomiting worms or other such slithering critters, including *The Boxer's Omen* and the demented *Seeding of a Ghost* (both 1983), which feature characters vomiting eels and worms, respectively. The latter film also features an exploding toilet, a man enthusiastically gobbling what he believes to be coconut pudding but is actually brains, and a woman giving birth to a *Deadly Spawn*-like monster that proceeds to eat the guests. Although Shaw Brothers '80s horror consists of multiple must-see freakshows, by then, the films had moved away from bug-related body horror as a central theme. The earlier, infamous *Killer Snakes* (1973) dealt with people being terrorized and killed by trained venomous snakes and other reptiles, but there is no puking-of-snakes to be seen.

However, it was not the Shaw Brothers who took this bizarre idea to its extreme. Two obscure films (though notorious among Chinese horror aficionados) would go above and beyond what any other preceding film had dared: Jen-Chieh Chang's *The Devil* (1981) and Keith Li's *Centipede Horror* (1982).

Centipedes had played a role in Shaw Brothers horror, usually chopped up and mixed into a potion, which would be subsequently gulped down by some hapless victim seeking mystical protection. But in *Centipede Horror*, the creatures are front and center. For anyone who has ever been alarmed at the sight of an inch-long specimen scurrying away, this is not the movie for you. The centipedes that attack in this film are 6 to 8 inches long (not even close to the biggest they can get in nature), and there are dozens—if not hundreds—of them racing across floors, up walls, and into a bed where an unsuspecting couple is making out. These actors were hopefully well-paid.

A young woman wants to take a trip with a girlfriend to an area of the country where her family is not permitted to go. Her brother agrees to not tattle on her to their mother as long as she wears a magical amulet for protection.

While she and her friend are

Oh, the Centipede Horror! (aka Wu gong zhou, 1982) (Copyright Yu Enterprises. All Rights Reserved.)

buying some grass jelly (?) from a street cart, the old man serving them can't help but notice that the amulet is the family crest of a lineage that did some great wrong to his ancestors. Turns out he is an evil magician and tending the street cart is just his day job. He decides to set upon the duo the centipede curse. Seems like a harsh penalty for being in the wrong place at the wrong time, but the prospect of selling grass jelly to tourists all day is bound to make anyone get up on the wrong side of the bed.

Later, sis decides the amulet is cramping her style and removes it. While she and her companion are answering nature's call in the woods, they are attacked by giant centipedes. In the hospital, her brother is horrified to find out that not only has his sister died a horrible, painful death, covered with welts and bruises, but live centipedes are crawling out from under her skin.

His sister having died under what can only be called mysterious circumstances, big brother decides to get to the bottom of her fate and brings his girlfriend along for the ride. Their investigation includes meeting an exorcist who cures a possessed girl (with the help of his ghost assistants) by making her vomit blood and scorpions. The exorcist recognizes that the sister died from the centipede curse, which makes the scorpion curse look like a walk in the park. He refers them to a magician who might be able to help, and he provides them with a snake venom-filled amulet for protection.

Unfortunately, the evil sorcerer has the girlfriend under his spell and instructs her to seduce the brother and remove the amulet. As a surreal and thrilling magic battle begins between the two sorcerers that involves reanimated chicken carcasses and remote-control fireballs, hundreds of centipedes descend upon the room in which the two lovebirds are getting it on. The slithering critters cover the floor, creep into bed with them, and attack. The brother leaps about like a kid avoiding imaginary lava, while the magicians' battle comes to a head, ultimately leading to the film's infamous scene in which the girlfriend vomits live centipedes (twice).

Centipede Horror's climax outdoes the cockroach-swarmed finale of *Creepshow*

in the skin-crawl factor as the two actors (and presumably the crew) are besieged by live centipedes, each close to a foot long, each with 30 or so needle-like legs, and each with a painful, venom-filled bite. How this scene was filmed is a mystery for the ages, as is how the actress was talked into stuffing live centipedes into her mouth and then spitting them out (actually, the spitting part probably didn't take much convincing).

A fast-paced, well-made chiller with a dark sense of humor, *Centipede Horror* is worth finding and checking out (It is currently being screened theatrically by American Genre Film Archive in a 2K scan from the only 35mm print in existence). But while it has a visceral sense of mean-spirited horror to it (despite never taking itself very seriously), a Taiwanese horror film was released a year earlier that reigns supreme to this day as cinema's ultimate bug-puking extravaganza.

The Devil more closely follows the soap opera schlock approach of the *Black Magic* films, but it makes the vomiting of worms more or less the running theme. Sure, there's intrigue, family drama, some nonsense about a real-estate swindle, and, of course, Ding Dong the bellboy getting in everybody's business.

Oddly light-hearted in general, *The Devil* seems to have constructed the most threadbare (yet convoluted) of plots for no other reason than to get to the next gore-drenched scene, and all of these scenes feature more wriggling things and multicolored ooze erupting from multiple unfortunate victims than any other film this writer has seen.

A woman is bashed in the face with a rock during a creepy opening scene, her purse is stolen, and she is left for dead. She isn't taking being killed lying down, however, and repeatedly comes back as a disfigured phantom to haunt anyone who might have had anything to do with her death.

Meanwhile, a witch cuts open a stricken man's bloated, pulsating stomach to reveal his intestines are infested with worm and maggots, causing him to rot from the inside out. She gives his guts a good cleaning by physically scooping out handfuls of worms and then makes him drink a remedy made from a (real) pulverized snake and various herbs and spirits. She instructs him on how close he was to death and how to go about recovering before he spits up more worms.

Soon after, a man is getting drunk in a bar where an instrumental version of Billy Joel's "The Stranger" is playing over the sound system. His bottle of hooch is spiked with...something. On his way home, he is terrorized by the face-bashed woman's ghost and subsequently twists and screams in agony on the sidewalk as worms, maggots, eels, centipedes, blood, pus, and bile erupt from his skin and mouth. The scene goes on and on and, were it not so morbidly revolting, might be comical after a few moments.

Other victims, all of whom had something or other to do with the ghostly woman's death (I've seen the film multiple times and still can't figure out how all these characters fit into the plot), suffer a similar fate. One is put out of his worm-excreting misery by kindly onlookers, who decide the best course of action is to tie him up and set him on fire. Why make it quick when you know the chances of getting to see this again are slim to none?

But the brains behind the real-estate swindle gets the brunt of the curse when the family who owns the hotel he is trying to gain control of find out. See, the mother is the witch who performed the worm removal earlier in the film. She agrees to inflict the curse upon the grifter, and he spends a solid five minutes of screen time upchucking worms and black slime. Fun!

Despite the confusing story and awful screenplay, the film is stylishly shot, with lots of green and red filters and shots in which the camera appears to be millimeters away from puddles of worm-ridden putrescence. If you're willing to forgo plot and dialogue in favor of outlandish scenes of gore, *The Devil* might be up your alley.

Revenge is a dish best served cold, and even better when it comes with slimy, writhing creatures eating your enemy from the inside out. We've all been wronged, and the idea of crucifying an abusive mother with kitchen utensils, making an evil government agent explode all over a room, or sicking your army of trained rats on your jerk boss has a certain appeal. But why not go that extra mile and really make them pay for what they've done (or what their ancestors did, if you're partial to grudges)?

Be nice to people. You never know who has access to rotting flesh, breast milk, and snake juice. Do you want to find out?

Note about Justin's own worm horror:

Should there be any doubts that Justin Wingenfeld knows his stuff about worm and larval horror, look no further than his own directorial debut, *Skin Crawl* (2007), released by Camp Motion Pictures. In a gleefully ghoulish and stylish homage to EC Comics and Italian gore films, a murdered woman returns from the grave, dripping maggots from her mouth, to take hideous revenge on her husband, his mistress, and the two men who killed her. One victim in particular winds up regurgitating the wigglies in a singularly grotesque manner that will challenge all stomachs! *Skin Crawl* stars Julian Wells, Kevin G. Shinnick, John Paul Fedele, Debbie Rochon, and the great Michael R. Thomas (doing a marvelous impression of Reggie Nalder's character in 1970's *Mark of the Devil*).

CROCODILE (1980)
by Pete Chiarella

Did you ever see a movie that you really can't explain? *Crocodile* falls into that category. Obviously a *Jaws* rip-off, it was a Thailand import from Herman Cohen and was produced by Dick Randall, who picked up many Far East horror and exploitation films to distribute. Both Randall and Cohen made edits to the film. Being that I'm a sucker for reptiles in general, I saw this on 42nd Street back in the day, and it seems about a week after that it was out on Thorn EMI Home Video. I recommend using liquor, weed, or any CDS to get through this film.

So, we have a doctor on vacation with his family—a family that, I might add, he's not paying much attention to. The film opens with a typhoon or something. We see shots of a real croc opening its eyes. Either volcanic activity or a nuclear bomb mutated this thing to Godzilla-like proportions. In other scenes, it's smaller and you're hard-pressed to identify real crocs from the "fake" one. We see a lot of people knocked over by water.

The doctor's wife, daughter, and friend are eaten by the croc. No fanfare—they just get pulled under. Three people in less than two minutes; I'd say he was hungry. Now we get an extended period of boredom as the doctor, the boyfriend of the friend, and a crusty fisherman figure out what's next. The croc attacks a village. We see cyclonic whirlpools, footbridges collapsing beneath peoples' feet, and others spitting up

blood when getting chomped or their insides crushed by the croc.

With the cinematography, you don't know if a miniature village is being destroyed or a real one is being leveled with high-pressure water cannons. Yes, it's that crazy. When the croc attacks, a siren-like noise accompanies it. The next attack has more carnage—a guy swimming away with chewed-off legs, floating body parts, more spurting blood.

More boring crap follows until the croc eats some girls swimming. We see blood flow. One girl goes feet-first down its gullet. Next is an obvious cut to a different scene. Now we have skin divers laying out what looks to be a big bear trap anchored to a tree. The divers get eaten, the croc's tail gets caught in the trap, and the tree gets ripped out and flung into the jungle. Patrons of the theater are freaking out during this.

This scene features grainy stock footage of a real swimming croc that doesn't match the film's normal footage at all. Some naked little boys swim and the croc has them for dinner. It then attacks another village—or maybe it's the same village with different shots. A lot of Westerners are in the crowd scenes. "Hey, you guys on vacation? Cool. Want to be in a movie?"

Finally, the three men take off in a boat to hunt the beast down (think the S. S. *Minnow* with a harpoon gun). They drop chum in the water to attract the croc. Seriously, it just ate a water buffalo; like the ass end of a dead fish is going to attract it?

Adding to another lengthy stretch of boredom, a reporter, Peter, shows up. The minute he speaks, you wish him dead. The croc attacks at night. It jumps over the boat twice. The skipper is eaten while the other three are trapped below deck. Now we have a daylight confrontation and another guy gets eaten. The reporter wraps himself with dynamite and does a kamikaze drive down the beast's throat. There's a big explosion and everyone dies. The end.

Yeah, continuity isn't this film's strong point. The attack scenes are fun, but there is zero character development. After repeated viewings, I'd say it really needed a good editor. "The End" pops up right after the big explosion. It looked like they lost a few minutes of the print and the distributor just slapped this on after the film ran out. VCI put out the DVD, but now I'm told that some company is going to give it the Blu-ray treatment. Whoopie!

"Never smile at a crocodile..." (Copyright Chaiyo Productions. All Rights Reserved)

QUARANTINE 2020: DOUBLE FEATURE OF ANIMAL ATTACKS!

by Dr. Rhonda Baughman

This extra *EN* issue seems appropriate within current quarantine context for multiple reasons: Movies offer comfort, our beloved animals offer comfort (in quarantine, not even the most apocalyptically imaginative among us predicted movies and pets offer hope when little else can), and, honestly, *everything* in 2020 feels like it's attacking. I feel attacked from every side.

A double feature of animal attacks feels therapeutic in a way, like my subconscious believes we deserve to be consumed and devoured. Watching this double feature is my quiet answer to anyone who has embraced the lunacy like the fictional Clay Easton from Bret Easton Ellis's *Less Than Zero* (1987) has done when he says, "...I realize that the money doesn't matter; that all that does is that I want to see the worst." It feels like the collective unconscious is saying this relentlessly, repetitively. (They can stop now. We've seen the worst. Let's move forward.)

Speaking of the unconscious and its dynamo synchronicity, David Benatar virtually predicted this issue with his spear-in-the-gut op-ed for *The New York Times*: "Our Cruel Treatment of Animals Led to the Coronavirus."[1] The article lays out the basics of zoonotic disease and species barrier-jumping and is quite direct when blame is placed at human feet: We butcher and mistreat, we torture and exhaust. *We get in the way*. Maybe, just maybe, the animals are attacking right now in a new way, and the virus is their new weapon. And who could be more vengeful and ready to take out the human race than sharks—those sleek, hardcore assassins of the ocean that we love to make movies about?

Sharks have become increasingly intelligent and vengefully cinematic as the years have progressed. And movies are simply reflections of how we live. So, who's to say animals turning on us in real life won't continue to happen? (And maybe, the darkest attack of all is already in progress as I write this. Fucking Benatar op-ed.) Man versus sharks. Predator against predator. We love this genre. Sharks are smart, and I suspect they know how much we love to invade the

---

1   www.nytimes.com/2020/04/13/opinion/animal-cruelty-coronavirus.html

to create tension. Much of the time, it succeeds for me, because being trapped/lost underwater is a nightmare that follows many of us from childhood to adulthood, so why not add a clever killer shark for extra terror?

What's with the sustained interest in the claustrophobic-trapped-underwater-we're-running-out-of-air-humans-don't-actually-belong-in-the-ocean-and-here-comes-a-shark genre anyway? I'll get personal and specific. Why do I watch movies in that genre? I know it gives me heart palpitations. I know people are gonna die and CGI sharks aren't all that scary. So, what is the specific appeal? Comfort? Maybe. Is it as simple as universal conflicts like man versus self and man versus nature? Possibly. But there's another question humans seemingly never grow tired of, and so the answer is closer to WWID(ITHS) ("What would I do [in this hopeless situation]?"). I must ponder (and ponder in an endless, circular manner, because it's comforting)![3]

I first noticed this WWID(ITHS) thought-train in *Uncaged* when SISTER 1, presumed dead, dramatically reappears, very much alive, to catch the wrist of SISTER 2 right before vast watery darkness consumes her! This scene repeats near the end in a swapped placement scenario: SISTER

deep. We're so fucking invasive that even though we must rely completely on extensive equipment to breathe underwater, we do it anyway so we can bust a move right through a shark's living room. Why? Because we're No. 1![2] Obviously, we think this even in places where we don't belong.

So, hypothetically, if I were a blind shark and some spoiled humans (archaeologists and their equally bratty kids and friends) disrupted my ancient Mayan habitat, I'd be toothy, pissed, and ready to take some juicy thigh meat with me too. And that's just what happens to the adventurous group in *47 Meters Down: Uncaged* (2019). They swim and plot and plan, and the film jump scares and tries

---

2   This is clearly an example of SOC 101's ethnocentrism.

3   Ah-ha. See what I did there? Comfort, circled back to comfort…? Seriously, this fuckin' quarantine, man, even has introverted me half-crazy.

2, safely aboard a boat, returns to the treacherous waters to save SISTER 1. My first thought was (since I don't have a sister), *What would my BFF and I do in these situations?* Would we battle seemingly insurmountable odds to rescue one another—twice? While the answer is yes, of course, many a yes—about halfway through the original first scenario analysis, I thought: *Ah, fuck it. My BFF and I would never go scuba diving in the first damn place.* One snorkel adventure in the Bahamas pre-9/11 was enough for me. Ten minutes of *Wow, pretty shell. Great. Clear water. So nice. Ah, little fishy. So cute. What the fuck is that looming darkness right there? Oh, an undersea shelf with a 2-mile drop-off? Cool. Bye!* and younger Rhonda flipped away to wait out that bullshit on the boat.

Uncaged isn't the best of the genres it represents (sharks, attacking animals, man versus animal/nature), but it sure as hell isn't the worst either. I'm sure it's wildly improbable anyone could top the *Jaws* series, but let's be real: All of you reading this right now could smoke a mountain of mediocre marijuana and chisel out scripts to defeat the *Sharknado* series. I found two high points in *Uncaged* right away: I immediately liked the music in the film. It has a poppy-without-being-overly-condescending opening number, and later, Roxette plays underwater while a veteran archaeologist is hard at work and jamming to some tunes. I jammed along. Secondly, teen girls can't stop screaming and victory woo'ing or even keep quiet in a life-or-death situation, and they need punished for such transgressions (e.g., shark snackers). Thus, I am there to witness the carnage, as all good carnage needs a witness. So, good, bad, goofy, or boring, I'm going to watch a killer-shark flick, as are many others, until we find the saturation point, *if* that point even exists.

After I bored myself (briefly) with shark movies on streaming platforms, I knew it was time to revisit one more

"That shark is such a dick!...It's right behind me, isn't it?"
(Copyright The Fyzz Facility. All Rights Reserved)

animal attack movie: *The Food of the Gods* (1976). This is writer/director/producer Bert Gordon's adaptation of the 1904 three-book sci-fi deluge by H.G. Wells. The opening quote from football dude clued me in right away that not only would I still love this film, but I would love it for reasons other than the gigantic chicken attack and the appearance by Ida Lupino:

> *"One of these days, the Earth will get even with Man for messing her up with his garbage. Just let man continue to pollute the Earth the way he is and Nature will rebel. It's gonna be one hell of a rebellion.... You'll never know when and where it's going to happen. And once it starts, you'll never know how and when it will stop." —Marjoe Gortner*

Whew. There's some mind-blowing synchronicity between the film and current events/the damn op-ed.

Although Gortner's Wiki is a deep rabbit hole I fell into, I did *not* buy his 1972 album, and I mercifully tuned back into the film, right at the part where a grumpy car couple blow past a pregnant woman on the side of the road because, who cares? They have grumpy-car-couple shit to do—no time for preggers. What the flick is trying to say is, well… it's possibly three things: humans are douchebags, we treat animals badly, and we're all going to suffer for that douchebaggery and animal mistreatment. The film is not wrong—and our current climate as I write this (mid-April 2020) shows me as much.

There's also not enough urgency in *The Food of the Gods*. I can hear this lack of urgency in the bored dialogue delivery and the very few screams in the first 40 minutes. The screams and "oh no" gasps pick up a little later in the film, but the delayed reaction of the film seems to mirror the ridiculously delayed reaction of our "leadership" to the current crisis. Maybe it's just me, but if I were shooting giant wasps and fending off overgrown cluckers (and in charge of a country), I might let out a war cry or grunt (or a yelp at the very least) to show some investment in the fight. This might just be indicative of the shlocky B-films of the big-creature genre from the '70s, OR...OR—and bear with me here—the same lack of urgency I see and hear in *Gods* is the *same* fucking lack of urgency I see and hear currently in a ruling class (with shitty, hack, yakking celeb heads thrown in) that seems to not care much about the ever-rising virus death toll. "Well, *I'm* not sick, so who fuckin' cares?" Ironically, in a round of obvious symbolism, both the film and current events do give viewers the cliched biblical quote, dialogue about money and toilet paper, and big white rat leading the pack, making this double feature a synchronistic feast for my battered senses.

7608-09 LAST STAND -- Mrs. Skinner (IDA LUPINO) flails desperately at a voracious rodent grown gigantic as a result of consuming a mysterious substance oozing from the ground on her remote island farm in American International's horror-drama based on the H. G. Wells' classic "The Food Of The Gods." Written, produced and directed by Bert I. Gordon, the film also stars Marjoe Gortner, Pamela Franklin and Ralph Meeker.
(c) American International Pictures 1976   All Rights Reserved

MANEATING MOTIFS: THE LONGEVITY OF SHARK ATTACK 3: MEGALODON

by Ally Melling

Coming soon to your aquarium.
(All photos this section Copyright Martien Holdings A.V.V. All Rights Reserved.)

Dunnn. Dunnn-dunnn. Dun-dun. Dun-dun dun-dun.

Only a few weeks after *Jaws* was released in the summer of 1975, everyone knew what that sound meant. Steven Spielberg himself has openly admitted that composer John Williams's musical motif played a pivotal role in *Jaws* becoming a blockbuster phenomenon. When those two notes play, the viewer knows Amity Island's great white maneater is present…and hungry. Almost 50 years later, every prankster on a coastal vacation still hums that famous theme to unnerve a fellow swimmer.

Cut to the 2000s, particularly the early days of video-sharing sites like YouTube and Vimeo. Memes and viral videos gained steam as more and more people began to join social media platforms. Among those shared were a few similar video clips of a giant shark gobbling down a boat, a life raft, a jet ski—all via some *particularly* terrible special effects. So laughable were these clips that they were soon widely shared, garnering millions upon millions of views. The question soon rose in every commenter's mind: Could these increasingly popular clips truly be from a *real* film?

You bet your ass they are. And that film is goddamn genius.

That said, some slight suspension of disbelief is needed to recognize the accidental brilliance of *Shark Attack 3: Megalodon* (2002). As the viewer, you must prepare to enter an alternate version of reality, and I don't just mean one where *Carcharocles megalodon* has survived millions of years to terrorize contemporary seas. It's a reality so inconsistent with our own that viewers leave the film more than a little baffled by what they've just seen.

But really, the world of *Shark Attack 3: Megalodon* isn't so bad. Everyone is overly smiley, laughy, jokey, winky, and adamant about everything they say. Here, boats can be driven using only one throttle, Maine lobsters have migrated to the Pacific coast of Mexico and nailed themselves to the ocean floor for easy catching, and (perhaps a geekier red flag) fiber optic cables carry and bleed electricity instead of light. Digital cameras can instantly transmit perfect, white-background images to your computer without cables or Wi-Fi, and buckets of water mixed with cherry Jell-O powder pass for chum. The sex is cringy but amazing (even in the ocean [*Ouch!*]), and the sex banter is equally on par.

My watch!

Allow me to set the scene of this utopian but shark-infested world. Lifeguard and beach patrolman Ben Carpenter (John Barrowman [*Arrow*]) finds a large shark tooth lodged in a communications cable off the coast of the Playa del Rey, Mexico, resort where he works. In his quest to identify the species of the "mystery shark" (or "mistery shark," as his Web posting says in one scene), Ben catches the attention of paleontologist Cat Stone (*Grimm*'s Jennifer "Jenny" McShane, in a whole different role than the one she played in the original *Shark Attack* [1999]). Cat recognizes the tooth as belonging to the supposedly extinct megalodon species. After some banter with a museum security guard (who is obviously the brother of someone on the production company's board of directors), Cat travels to Mexico disguised as a marine biologist looking to study the "rare shark" owner of Ben's tooth. However, when all hell breaks loose and tourists start getting chomped, Cat comes clean with Ben and agrees to help him hunt the baby meg. They are successful, but things soon go from bad to worse when the mama mega-meg shows up and begins devouring watercraft. It turns out that the villainous head of Apex Communications (a corporation with a logo that would get any graphic designer fired) knew

Jenny McShane and Captain Jack Harkness.

his intercontinental communications cabling was bringing things up from the Challenger Deep Trench. Desperate, Ben and Cat team up with ex-Navy man and obvious Bush/Cheney enthusiast Chuck (Ryan Cutrona [*The Last Boy Scout*]) to battle both the mammoth meg and the evil corporation that threatens to serve more tourists up on a silver platter.

As you can see, the story itself doesn't offer any standout fresh takes on a subgenre that's been chewed to death over decades. Dutifully, it follows a common theme of countless "animals attack" films: Evil corporation/mayor/military branch meddles with nature (or simply dismisses nature's primitive power), and when nature retaliates, people die. Needless to say, *Shark Attack 3: Megalodon* isn't a film that stands out for its ingenious plot. In addition, the mise-en-scène is mediocre, and the score is neither diegetically clever nor even very original.

The lasting power of *Shark Attack 3: Megalodon* lies in the perfect storm it embodies: a dumpster fire so bright and spectacular that the viewer cannot look away from the blaze. And in that magical combination of sloppy filmmaking, terrible scripting, and laughable post-production, the film finds its own low-budget immortality. Therein lies its enduring motifs.

Shark Attack 2 director David Worth (*Kickboxer*) was brought back to steer this third installment for Millennium Films. However, *Shark Attack 3: Megalodon* would have nothing to do with the mutant-shark storyline of the second film. Instead, *Shark Attack* series screenwriters Scott Devine and William Hooke looked to *New York Times* best-selling author Steve Alten's book *Meg* (later more legally adapted by Warner Bros. to become the 2018 box office success *The Meg*) for "inspiration." To their credit, however, Devine and Hooke only really took the basic premise of a megalodon emerging from a trench and eventually battling a small submarine. Everything else is straight from their *inventive* imaginations... except when it's not.

Indeed, *Shark Attack 3: Megalodon* is loaded with subtle nods (and outright headbangs) to *Jaws*, *Deep Blue Sea*, and other predacious predecessors. One scene, for instance, features a man playing fetch on the beach with his dog (ala *Jaws* lovers—"Here, Pipit!"), though, in this version, the man becomes the lunch, with his dog the only witness. However, as if to say, "No, you were right—I was thinking of *Jaws*," Worth finishes the scene with a shot of the man's severed leg drifting to the ocean floor.

Another scene features the baby meg busting through the hull of a ship and lunging at the two main heroes. In this world of favorable physics, however, the hull doesn't flood while the assault takes place. Shotguns can also be fired after soaking for 15 minutes—a lucky break for viewers, lest we be robbed of the one-liner, "You're extinct, fucker!" (which, yes, falls a bit short of "Smile, you son of a bitch!").]

Speaking of *Jaws* "homages," some part of the Worth's post-production crew thought it would be the greatest idea ever to take Spielberg's use of *The Creature from the Black Lagoon*'s Gil Man roar (aka the moan of dying trucks [*Duel*] and sinking fins [*Jaws*]) and turn it up to 11. Not only do the sharks in *Shark Attack 3: Megalodon* roar *a lot*, they growl and grunt and gurgle with indigestion. Indeed, one of the kill scenes is just a close-up of shark skin in bloody water with roars and half-hearted human screams overlaid.

Stock footage is really the key component behind most of the *Shark Attack 3: Megalodon*'s most unforgettable sequences—those recurring scenes shared again and again by the amused and the stupefied. Obviously, no logical viewer would have expected Millennium Films to shell out the kind of budget a mechanical shark would require (And what company would for a third installment meant to go straight to video?), and lord knows the infamous issues Spielberg and his crew encountered with "Bruce" while filming Universal's classic. The cheapest workaround was clearly to use stock footage of great whites for megs and worry about the details later. After all, Spielberg himself had done it for scenes in *Jaws'* second act.

The result is the best of the worst (or maybe the worst of the best). The two megs are reduced to a series of Discovery Channel "Shark Week" specials, with the close-up kills (when they're actually shown) either cleverly reduced to clips of sharks being fed fabric-wrapped meat, subbed for rubber jaws, or altogether CGI'd. Of the three, the third is the most popular and widely shared among the masses. The clips of the mega-meg devouring Cat's crew, a small boat, a life raft full of people, a plummeting villain, and the main bad guy (as he rides a jet ski into the shark's waiting jaws) are all basically the same up-close, sometimes-flipped stock shot of a wide-mouthed great white breaking the surface. The CGI used to facilitate all this gobbling is so bad that it makes *Die Another Day*'s tsunami-surfing look like damned *Inception*. (Though, to be totally fair, far worse CGI shark fare has been released over the past 18 years.) Still, in this cheap, lazy, repetitive way, these scenes have become a distinct motif recognized by millions.

Of course, the other timeless, widely shared bit of *Shark Attack 3: Megalodon* doesn't involve the megs: It's all thanks to the flair of the film's main star. In case you didn't know, John Barrowman is a goddamn national treasure (Follow him on any social media platform and you'll see). Mostly likely, you are way ahead of me and didn't discover him by watching this film in your 20s or seeing his fabulous rendition of *La Cage aux Folles*' gay anthem, "I Am What I Am," on YouTube. As a non-Whovian, I'm told his portrayal of recurring character Captain Jack Harkness on *Dr. Who* stole the show, so much so that a spin-off, *Torchwood*, ran for four seasons with Harkness front and center. Barrowman isn't given much to work with in *Shark Attack 3: Megalodon* (with such clever lines as "Sharks are always biting things" and "We found a guy's leg near where he was playing Frisbee with his dog"), and admittedly, his performance is pretty campy. But that pre-Harkness charm and charisma definitely shine through, to the point where Barrowman is almost more of a joy to watch than the unbelievable CGI.

And, of course, there's the line Barrowman matter-of-factly improvised that got left in the film. You know—the one that's been

41

viewed millions of times in itself: "But you know, I'm really wired. What do you say I...take you home and eat your pussy."

With this one line alone, Barrowman's Ben becomes indispensable to the chaos that comprises *Shark Attack 3: Megalodon*'s utopia. Still, there are numerous other memorable/baffling highlights scattered here and there throughout the film. Thanks to the varying shark footage and CGI inconsistencies, the sizes of both predators change constantly from shot to shot, as does the size of their jaws compared to the teeth Ben keeps acquiring. At one point, the baby meg takes a parasailer on a terrifying ride before bringing her down for dinner (a scene no doubt dreamed up when the crew got its hands on some footage of a shark with a rope in its mouth). Later, in the most unarguably out-of-place scene in the whole film, Ben and Cat go to a church to pray before doing battle with the mega-meg.

Some of the film's events leave the viewer asking the important questions. Where did they find all these gorgeous extras willing to show their immaculate bosoms? Why is everyone except the three leads so poorly dubbed? For that matter, why is the entire supporting cast and crew Russian? Did the cinematographer just not *know* how to film close-ups and medium shots while a boat is in motion?

But I digress, these questions are unimportant in such a special reality. Years ahead of the shark-cheese wave of the 2010s (*Sharknado*, *Snow Shark*, *Three-Headed Shark Attack*, etc.), *Shark Attack 3: Megalodon* was made to be enjoyed for what it is: not a straight-to-video horror movie that's secretly good, but a film so unintentionally and unapologetically terrible that it achieves a whole other level of perfection. Viewers worldwide have recognized this, even if they've never actually seen the entire film. Just the 1:04 clip[1] where mega-meg sinks its teeth into bad guys, Sea-Doos, and the 1 percent currently has almost 60 million views. Meanwhile, Barrowman's straight-faced entreaty has nearly 3 million.[2]

In this way, *Shark Attack 3: Megalodon* has achieved cult status for far different reasons than *Jaws* and its tell-tale theme. Flagrancy is *Megalodon*'s motif, abomination its language. But really, isn't that the best way to survive the test of time?

Genius, I say.

---

1   "Shark Attack 3: Megalodon." *YouTube*, uploaded by Jon Harvey, 4 April 2007. https://youtu.be/1nzd0R_OeOc

2   "Shark Attack 3 – That Famous Line." *YouTube*, uploaded by Blaithyn, 13 Feb. 2007. https://youtu.be/w1XOfHax6Q8

ROAR: WHEN ANIMALS ATTACK FILMMAKERS

Roar (1981) is about Hank (writer/director/producer/lunatic Noel Marshall), an American conservationist living on a Tanzanian nature preserve, ostensibly to study the behavior of big cats. His loving family supports him, but he's at odds with the local government, which believes the big cats are a menace to society, what with their hunting and mauling and smoking and loud music. Before long, it's everybody and their guns against Hank and his lions, tigers, cheetahs, panthers, and one short-haired tabby named Fuckatron. (I may have made the last part up.)

If I seem glib in my synopsis, it's because it doesn't matter what *Roar* is about. Nothing in the movie, from its plot to its shoot-and-run photography, is as batshit insane as how this movie got made.

A Hollywood agent who was married to Tippi Hedren, Noel Marshall made his fortune repping William Peter Blatty and subsequently co-producing *The Exorcist*. While shooting the 1970 adventure film *Satan's Harvest*, Hedren and Marshall observed an abandoned house overtaken by a pride of lions. Poaching

had driven the big cats closer to civilization. On the advice of animal trainer Ron Oxley (who clearly did not have their best interests in mind and told them that to understand big cats, they had to live with one), Hedren and Marshall adopted a male lion named Neil and brought him to live with them in their Sherman Oaks home. This was the subject of a popular '71 photospread in *LIFE* magazine (photographed by Michael Rougier).

It's more fun than it looks. (Copyright Film Consortium. All Rights Reserved)

But you know what they say about owning lions: You can't stop at one. More big cats were added, illegally, to the family.

To bring awareness to the need for conservation of African wildlife, Marshall began working on a screenplay. It would be equal parts adventure story, conservation information, horror movie, and Mack Sennett slapstick comedy. It would star Marshall, Hedren, and their children, which included Melanie Griffith among their numbers. And they could shoot the film on their Soledad Canyon property because it totally looked like Tanzania! Even better, Marshall could use all the money he made on *The Exorcist* to fund it.

For those of you unfamiliar with the animal husbandry of large, wild apex predators, a lion isn't the same kind of animal as a tiger or cheetah. There is a reason these animals don't live near each other. Or near humans. Shooting began in 1976, and by the time production wrapped, somewhere between 70 and 100 cast and crew members were injured on set. In addition, 14 lions and tigers died as a result of airborne disease. Safety measures seemed to consist of the words "Freeze!" and "Run!"

Because of the unpredictable nature of six dozen jungle creatures, which, at this point, also included a bull elephant (Because why the fuck not?), *Roar* became an improvisational film. Cast and crew would sit around waiting for the animals to do something (aside from eating the filmmakers, presumably). When the animals didn't, or they did something he didn't like, Marshall would scream at the crew. From the attitudes of the cast and crew, Marshall's behavior seems to have been forgiven as his nature—no more able to be contained than the big cats.

The most famous horror stories include cinematographer Jan de Bont getting scalped by a lion, requiring 220 stitches, and becoming so traumatized that he made *Speed* decades later. Griffith had her head damn near swallowed, and it was feared she'd lose an eye, requiring the reconstructive surgery that would later attract Antonio Banderas. Hedren was bitten so badly that teeth touched her skull.

One of the lead lions, Togar, caught assistant director Doron Kauper in the throat and jaw; clawed his chest, legs, scalp; and then tried to pull off one of his ears after Kauper unintentionally cued an attack.

Marshall himself almost lost an arm, was bitten through his hand, and contracted gangrene so many times that he put it on his résumé as a "special skill." He claimed that he "willed" the gangrene from his body in order to continue.

Son and actor John Marshall told journalist David Onda, "I would try to be in the scenes with Tippi and Melanie because they felt better when I was nearby. We grouped together as a family. Not that we thought dad was really trying to kill us, but it really seemed like he was out for us for some reason."

"This was probably one of the most dangerous films that Hollywood has ever seen," remarked Hedren herself. "It's amazing no one was killed."

This isn't even taking into consideration the Aliso Canyon flood that destroyed much of the property. As a result, 15 lions and tigers escaped through collapsed fencing, and three lions, including lead lion Robbie, were shot and killed by local law enforcement. Marshall replaced the late Robbie with Zuru and thought audiences wouldn't notice!

It would take another five years before *Roar* was released...in the U.K. and Australia. *Roar* was not distributed in the U.S. Hedren has blamed greedy distributors for this, claiming studios wanted "the lion's share" of profits (no pun intended, I assume). Marshall and Hedren had intended the proceeds to fund the animals' much-deserved retirement. Instead, the couple divorced in 1982.

Roar wouldn't be seen in the U.S. until Drafthouse Films founder Tim League rediscovered it in 2015. Drafthouse promoted the film thusly: "No animals were harmed during the making of *Roar*. But 70 members of the cast and crew were!" League also kinda nailed it when he described it as the "snuff version of *Swiss Family Robinson*."

Hedren tried to regroup and refocus in 1983 by establishing the Roar Foundation and the Shambala Preserve, a sanctuary to house the animals after filming. A few years later, Griffith gave birth to Dakota Johnson, and the world has never forgiven her.

Roar was released on Blu-ray by Olive Films in 2015, and the extras do a good job of explaining the incoherent mess of a movie that is, without a doubt, one of the scariest movies ever made...at least according to those who made it.

GRIZZLY II: REVENGE

by Shawn Jones

In 1983 producers looking to make a quick buck by franchising the 1976 nature-gone-amok classic, *Grizzly*, shot (most of) a sequel. Everything that could go wrong did.

The animatronics didn't work, one of the producers went rogue, leaving the production without funds, and the film was left to collect dust for over 35 years. Producer Suzanne Nagy has finally cut the red tape and brought *Grizzly II: Revenge* back to life. Sort of.

Unfortunately, the negative is still sitting in a French vault, but Nagy *did* still have the 35mm workprint, as well as the audio masters. She's reassembled and remastered the film to play in a modern marketplace and the results are mixed. The new version of the film feels awfully padded. The workprint version was around 97 minutes. This version is loaded with stock footage and it's 74m with credits. There's probably a good half hour missing here. It's never boring, but it feels *very* disjointed without scraps of character work.

We open with a very-dodgy stock footage/CGI open where the cubs of the titular Grizzly are murdered by poachers. My biggest issue here is that the stock footage does not match well at all and pops up a few times during the already cut-within-an-inch-of-it's-life film. The novelty of a movie from 1983 being released for the 1st time in 2020 is enough; it doesn't need the distraction of modernized footage beyond putting the bear in the movie.

Still, it's pretty entertaining to see a young George Clooney, Laura Dern, and Charlie Sheen become the first victims of a bear attack. As news of the bear killings comes in, festival promoter Louise Fletcher hires expert tracker John Rhys-Davies, who often chews more scenery than the bear does campers. We also have a gang of poachers gumming up the works and greasing up the body count.

The B-Plot is the concert prep, and we're treated to an early performance by the wonderful Deborah Foreman as the daughter of the head ranger. There are several music numbers in full. One or two are earworms, but most fall flat, including a newly-shot performance by a band that likes to look directly into the camera.

Animal expert Deborah Raffin is

also on hand to slow down the capture of the Grizzly by trying to bring it in alive. This all comes to a head when the bear makes it's way to the concert. You can tell that they hadn't shot all of the ending because the action is a bit jumbled here, but the one day they got the animatronic to work is on display, and I've seen a worse finales. The production value of the concert is impressive (the stage was borrowed from the Rolling Stones).

Overall it's enjoyable enough and I'm glad this thing finally has a chance to be seen by a wide audience.

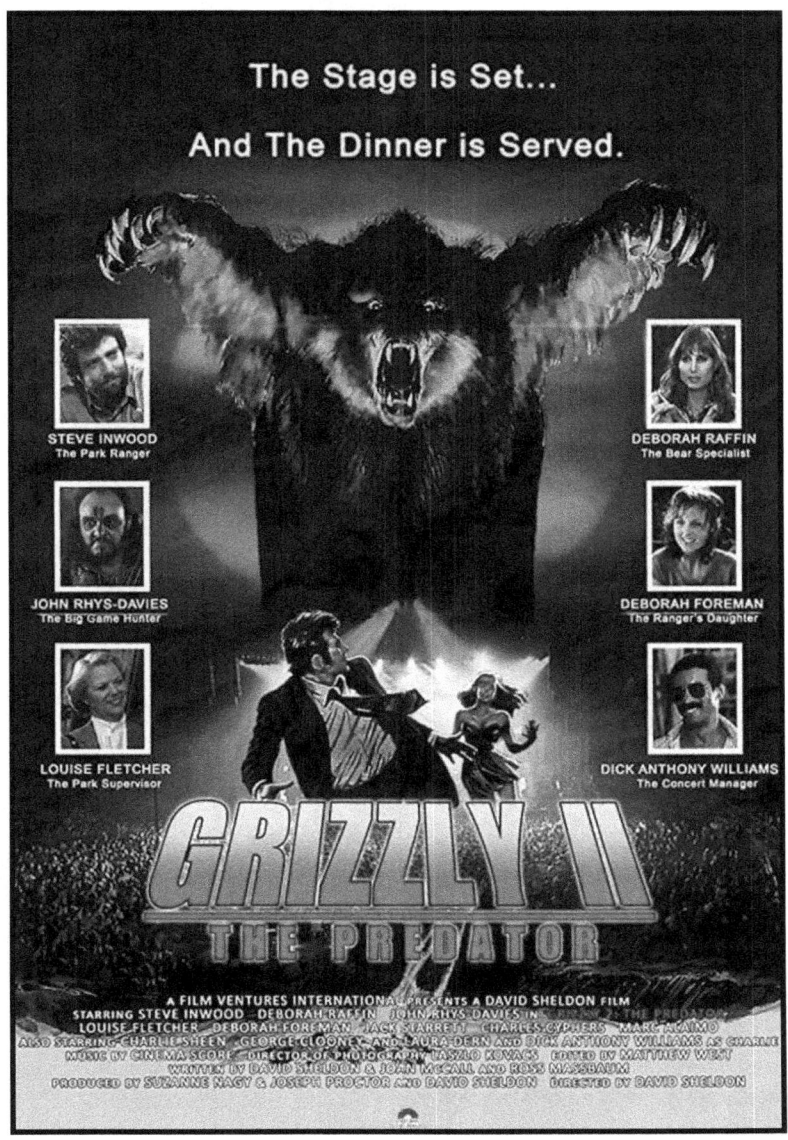

I WAS KILLED BY A 6-FOOT SCORPION AND LIVED TO TELL ABOUT IT

by Jason Paul Collum

It makes for a great story while swilling a vodka and water with friends. In November 2002, I worked varying roles on a little-known Full Moon venture that changed my life in many ways. One year earlier, I had been working as a writer and assistant editor at *Femme Fatales* magazine and had literally just been named the new editor-in-chief of its sister publication, *Cinefantastique*, when both were secretly sold to a new company and I was out of both jobs.

Over the ensuing three months, I was drowning in self-pity. I had succeeded in convincing the "King of Guerilla Filmmaking," J.R. Bookwalter (*The Dead Next Door*), to produce my scream queen documentary, *Something to Scream About*, so I should have been happy, yes? I wasn't.

A deep depression had set in. Then, in late October, I received a call from Bookwalter, who had become a close friend. Full Moon head Charlie Band had made a distribution deal with 20th Century Fox Home Video and wanted Bookwalter to lead the deal's first film, at that point titled *Stingers*. Eventually retitled twice, first as *Deadly Stingers* (which Bookwalter still labels *Deadly Stinkers*) and today as *Mega Scorpions*, the story follows residents of a halfway house battling toxically overgrown 6-foot scorpions. It stars Nicolas Read, Marcella Laasch,

Author Jason Paul Collum and director J.R. Bookwalter. (All photos courtesy Jason Paul Collum. All Rights Reserved.)

Darcey Vanderhoef, Sy Stevens, and pal.

Sewell Whitney, Sarah Megan White, and a plethora of B-movie faves, including Brinke Stevens (*The Slumber Party Massacre*), Jay Richardson (*Hollywood Chainsaw Hookers*), Trent Haaga (the *Killjoy* franchise), Jeff Dylan Graham (*Homesick*), Ariauna Albright (*Witchouse*), Lilith Stabs (*Bad Movie Police*), and pre-porn star Sunny Leone. Then, of course, there is me, in a very minor role as a nosy neighbor whose munched-up remains are discovered in the scorpion's lair.

My main role on set was as the assistant director. It was a stressful shoot. We filmed in the mountain home of Corman babe Robyn Harris (a.k.a. Gail Thackray) of *Sorority House Massacre II* "fame." Almost immediately, we had an oil spill in the driveway from a car-flipping sequence. The brand-new carpet in the master bedroom was stained. The Santa Ana winds paid us a nightly visit, knocking over lights, blowing actors around, and affecting sound in every outdoor sequence. The giant scorpions were more rubbery than expected (later fixed with CGI). We had an angry neighbor call the police because although we had a permit for some interior scenes at an alternate L.A. location, it didn't apply to the exterior—so she screamed and hollered every time Bookwalter called, "Action!" Then, there were the two scars I received: one emotional, one physical.

There's nothing more effective than public humiliation. The film's caterer, Orly Tepper, whom I refer to as "Ornery Temper," blew her lid after I asked the production assistants to move the craft service table since she had not yet arrived on set and we needed to film in the space she had set up. I assume, not knowing any better, they threw everything together in bags to move the food, and I was paying attention to other events. When she arrived and saw this, she tore up to me in her car, raging out at me in front of the entire crew— bulging eyes, red face, spit flailing from her mouth. Everyone stopped to watch. Then, she tore away, and our week was only half done. So, that made for fun times when every mealtime rolled around. I have never forgotten that moment.

The physical scar was something that occurred during my favorite part of the shoot: my gory discovery. To film it, I had to lie upside down in a cement ravine at a 45-degree angle with, really, nothing to dig my heels into to keep my body in place—for three hours. Now, this may sound horrible; I called it "challenging," because I really did enjoy it. There I was, soaked in blood—and Bookwalter made sure I was *soaked*, in my armpits, up my nose, down my crotch—FX wounds across my eye and face, with a live scorpion crawling on my chest...and it was awesome!

It wasn't until the next day when I was rubbing my upper stomach that I noticed something that felt like a rope under my skin. It went from my chest to my groin, and I could move it! Over the next several days, it moved constantly from the top to bottom of my torso. It didn't hurt, so I had to wait until I returned to Chicago. As it turns out, in doing the 45-degree angle stunt and arching my back for three hours, I had torn the fatty tissue between my skin and muscles. It took about four years for most of it to spread back out, but I still have a small area raised to the touch as a fun

JPC, Jennifer Kessler and Bookwalter.

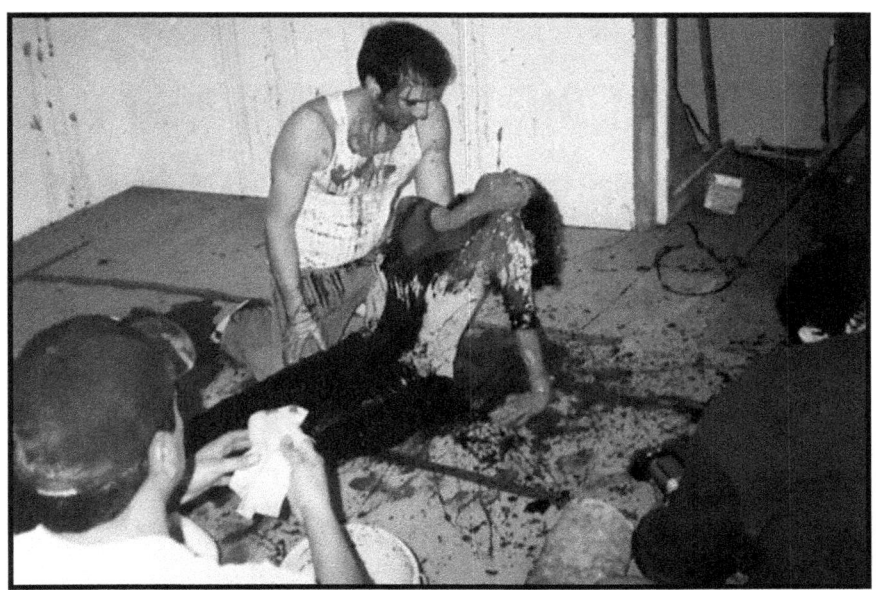

reminder. Still, it was totally worth it for the experience and my 3 minutes of screen time!

Mega Scorpions should not go down as this terrible experience, because there were also many wonderful experiences to come out of it. I got to meet Jay Richardson and Gail Thackray. I bonded even more with Bookwalter, whom I had come to see as a big brother. I proved to myself I could—overall—accomplish being a first assistant director on a professional film set. I fell into a short but passionate love affair. Most of all, I found that people trusted me to do my job, and it proved to me that I had more in me than what had already been with the magazines. It set me back on my way to my own film career.

In the year that followed *Mega Scorpions*, I completed *Something to Scream About* and my final camcorder movie, *5 Darks Souls, Part III*. I also published my first book, *Assault of the Killer B's*, and began preproduction on my passion project, *October Moon*. The love affair ended and the torn fat eventually healed, but I only recently realized that getting eaten and spit out by a 6-foot scorpion for a later meal was a significant turning point in my life. After the spiral I was in when the job was offered to me, the experience of *Mega Scorpions* allowed me to set and climb back toward my goals.

Side note: The film—a fun throwback to the monster bug movies of the 1950s—was released on television overseas as *Deadly Stingers* in 2005. Due to legal issues between Full Moon, its investors, and 20th Century Fox Home Video, the film didn't hit streaming services until 2013 as *Mega Scorpions*. It has never had an official disc release, although bootleg copies have been found at tables on the horror convention circuit.

WELL, I WONDER, WONDER WHO... WHO WROTE THE BOOK OF THE DEAD? OH, RIGHT...TOM SULLIVAN

Copyright (C) 2020 Tom Sullivan. All Rights Reserved.

Knee-deep in the quarantine and Tom Sullivan says what we've all been thinking: "I've actually been preparing for social distancing for decades now. I can't even begin to count how many films I have. I've filled about 70 boxes with just DVDs in paper folders. I have the Ray Harryhausen collection Blu-ray, so that's heaven for me right there. I can watch everything in 3-D."

But don't mistake entertainment for comfort. Tom's going a little south mentally, like the rest of us. The *Evil Dead* maestro is a mainstay at many horror cons, but especially at Cinema Wasteland[1], where he and "Bookbinder of the Dead" Pat Reese run the Tom Sullivan Movie Memorabilia Museum and Art Print Gallery in their own space across from Movie Room B. But with COVID-19 stampeding its way through the unmasked populace of the world, April Wasteland was only one of the many conventions forced to cancel in order to preserve safety. The problem is what will con life be like even after the lockdowns are lifted?

"I don't know if we're going to have any shows," Tom says, again voicing what many of us are thinking. "I'm thinking this is going to be really bad. Until recently, I'd go see Pat on Friday nights, and we'd watch a movie. And that's it for me socializing. I get to pet his cat for a couple of hours, and then I go home. I think we're going into a time of madness here."

There's plenty of anger and blame to go around, and it's hard not to

---

[1] Their first show in 2001 was Tom's first show.

All photos Courtesy and Copyright (C) 2020 Tom Sullivan. All Rights Reserved.

see the current situation—from the unstoppable virus, to the violent outsiders co-opting protests—as the apocalypse predicted by the Mayans. "I went through my old Facebook posts recently. I don't do this a lot, but I found the time. I wrote years ago that 2020 will be the last decade humans can recognize themselves as civilized. And I nailed it. I didn't think it would start on the day, though, but the shit hit the fan in January. And that's the good news!"

While it may be tempting to dismiss this as the all-too-common hyperbole of despair, let us not forget, at least on film, Sullivan has seen apocalypses before. He and Bart Pierce created one for the end of the seminal *Evil Dead*, in which the surviving Deadites transform, decompose, and explode all over the cabin and final girl Bruce Campbell.

But apocalypses are always more fun when they happen to others.

Fans of Tom's are already familiar with the documentary about him, *Invaluable*. While touring the Tennessee area in which *Evil Dead* was shot, Tom points out the window of the travel car and says, "And that's where the car was on fire." But the documentary never follows up on this story. Intrepid reporter that I am, the first question I ask is, "What is the car fire story?"

So, Tom took me back to 1978. "Everybody was at the cabin filming. I was at home base working on a makeup for Theresa [Tilly], I think. The dark veins coming out of her eyes. I had just finished applying that makeup to my own face when—*ding-dong!* And there's this grandma and grandpa standing there on my doorstep. I start saying, 'I'm sorry to scare you; we're making a movie. What can I help you with?'

"And they said, 'I don't know if you know, but there's a car on fire!' Right across the street, there was this large football-sized grass field that curved where the road went around it. And in the center of it is this relatively brand-new car, totally engulfed in flames. It had been torched. I immediately freaked out, thinking 'Oh my god, I'm going to find some of my friends dead.' I ran around the car—I could tell that nobody was inside. So, then, I called the police.

"So, I didn't hear anything for a couple of days. We're shooting all night, getting into bed around seven in the morning. Sure enough, 9 a.m.—*knock, knock, knock.* 'Uh, this is Officer Curley, can I speak to you?' And I get interviewed again and again. 'Did you know the elderly couple?' 'No. They were just driving by. I'm sure they had nothing to do with it.'

"And it turned out that some kid had just graduated, and his father had bought him a brand-new car. Some friends of his—or enemies of his—stole it and went on a joyride, and this was, like, a day after he just got the car. So, they stole it and then torched it. I know they caught the guys. And apart from the fines and the cost of the car, I'm sure they did some jail time. That's grand theft. Enh, it was what? Forty years ago?"

And that, dear friends, solves that mystery.

By now, the bardic tale of "The Making of *Evil Dead*" can be recited by any horror fan's smallest child. A small team of Michigan outsiders shot a backyard horror film to raise money for a feature. *Within the Woods* had Bruce Campbell ("Girls liked Bruce, so we put him in front of the camera. They didn't like us, so we stayed behind it," said Raimi.) discovering an old book and an "Indian dagger" that opens his body up to demonic possession. The giddy camerawork gave the larval *Evil Dead* a kinetic energy that producers enjoyed. Armed with money from a producer cadre of mostly dentists, Raimi, producer Rob Tapert, Campbell, Sullivan, Pierce, Josh Becker, the Professor, *and* Mary Ann all ventured south to Tennessee, took over a ramshackle cabin, and created what Stephen King called "the most ferociously original horror film I've ever seen." Thus: infamy.

Audiences flocked to the ambitious 16mm shocker, loving (and hating) every bloody minute. Five college chums vacation in a cabin in the woods, discover a book bound in human skin, ignore the screaming face that comprises the cover, and throw all caution to the wind. An accompanying tape recorder reveals the voice of a historian who, naturally, reads forbidden passages

Working on the "meltdown" climax of Evil Dead. (Copyright (C) 2020 Tom Sullivan. All Rights Reserved.)

out loud, thus unleashing Kandarian demons that possess bodies and can only be stopped by complete dismemberment.

The climax is often cited as the film's highlight: a multi-pass, in-camera, stop-motion sequence in which hell finds itself thwarted and the demonic corpses of Ash Williams's friends lose all molecular integrity in a spectacular way. It was a work of dedication that took hundreds of hours and is the standout sequence in a film that is overall exemplary in terms of gore, humor, and surreal terror.

The entire cast and crew went through the ringer, including long hours and basically making up the movie as they solved cinematic problems. Sullivan was responsible for the makeup and design of the Deadites. As the story goes, Raimi took one look at Sullivan's early designs and "threw them out." It's a story that normally irritates readers and listeners, but for Sullivan, it was just a part of making the best movie they could. "Yeah, I always took that in stride. I was just throwing things out there. They're supposed to be Sumerian demons, so my thought was, *Who knows Sumerian from Egyptian?* Egyptians like dogs, so I had one turn into a dog, another into a hawk, another into a—I think Betsy was going to be the snake. It would have been awful. I'm so glad we didn't go that way.

"Plus, he had a point that it was starting to look like *Planet of the Apes*. Plus, you know, you'd see mouths underneath the masks; we wouldn't have been able to afford special teeth. One had a beak. And they would have just been glued on, not whole-head masks. You'd have to have all the appliances as separate pieces, try to blend it—the designs would have added another three to four hours to the makeup process. Even the way I did it was four to five hours already. My thought was, *OK, instead of ripping off John Chambers, let's rip off Dick Smith*. Do more humanish things. So, I thought, *Let's make them demonic caricatures of the characters*. Betsy is idyllic, so let's make her a doll. I took a headcast from a female mannequin; made that white, ghostly mask from that; and cut the eyes out. The first makeup I did for the film was on Betsy, with the eyes radiating out. We filmed pretty much in sequential order. So, it was a couple of weeks in before we got to the makeup.

"I want to point out again, this was the late '70s. For a lot of self-taught makeup artists just entering the film industry, there wasn't a lot of information to draw from. In fact, there were two books that gave you a how-to on makeup: *Dick Smith's Do-It-Yourself Monster Make-Up Handbook* and Richard Carson's book, *Stage Makeup*, which is, of course, still a classic. That had all the basics—the materials, the application, basic face-casting stuff.... But it's so great to have actors make your stuff come alive. Betsy did that wonderfully, and after working on her face for five to six hours, and then she just knocks it out of the park. They had contact lenses made. The contacts were these old-fashioned things; they were hemispheres and had to be the full diameter of the eye. They had to have their eyes measured, which I'm told is uncomfortable. About the thickness of a quarter. I made Rob put them in (the actors' eyes)…I get squeamish. Don't tell me about your operation unless you wanna see me pass out. I can't take that stuff, and yet here I am, throwing guts in the audience's lap."

The first makeup shot was actually a simple one, and one of the last to be shot that night. "We were shooting that right at dawn. It had to be a night shot, so Sam picked the direction of the camera, and we put a black background behind it, so it wasn't nice blue sky behind her. Betsy is being dragged down the steps, screaming the whole way, reeling in pain. It was the first time we actually had a horror scene—you know, something genuinely scary. And I remember everyone was just speechless. We were all exhausted, it was the last shot of that night. Of course, Sam always left those kinds of things until the last second. But she nailed it. Got it in one take. It was so gratifying."

Most first films are family affairs. Either you're making your first film with your family, or your coconspirators become your family. Talk to any filmmaker about their first feature and you'll think you're reading letters home from Civil War soldiers. "It was just me and my battalion, facing a rain day without coverage…." I ask Tom if he has any specific memories of making *Evil Dead* that made it a family affair.

"When we were making *Evil Dead*, Gary Holt was our production manager, and his family invited us to Thanksgiving dinner. They cooked two huge turkeys. It was terrific. They couldn't have been sweeter folks. Now this is, like, the buckle of the Bible Belt, in eastern Tennessee.

I remember we sat down, and the grandmother of the household sits down next to Sam, who's Jewish, and says, 'So, are you able to get to church on Sundays when you're making your movie?'

"And Sam couldn't have been more diplomatic." Tom adopts the "Raimi voice" that all the *Evil Dead* folks lapse into when they want to "aw-shucks" the audience.[2] "'Well, we certainly try to, but it's difficult with the film schedule.' [*Laughs*] I don't recall that issue ever coming up.

"After the dinner, and it really was a feast, Mom couldn't have done better (and I helped Mom). But sometime during dinner, the cows had gotten out. We all went out and formed a big circle to corral the cows back into the fence. That was a lot of fun."

While film families rarely last—you hear similar stories from folks who'd worked on *Night of the Living Dead* who didn't go on to subsequent Romero features, for instance—the *Evil Dead* family wandered off in separate directions after the first film. Campbell, Raimi, and Tapert went on to *Evil Dead II*, for which Sullivan sculpted the book and dagger, but for a variety of reasons, wasn't present on set. Effects work went to the up-and-coming KNB EFX.

Just prior to *Evil Dead*, Tom had gotten involved in an ill-fated Lovecraft-inspired film titled *The Cry of Cthulhu*. Bill Baetz and David Hurd (a.k.a. Byron Craft) were behind the project and brought Sullivan aboard to contribute designs. He collaborated with Cary Howe to create maquettes

---

2   Pat Reese and Bruce Campbell do this. I've heard Ted Raimi do it as well…come to think of it, Lucy Lawless pulled this voice on me too.

of the creatures, photographing them against real backgrounds (in some cases, using rear projection to really make the sculptures come to life). Their hard work was showcased in *Starlog* and *Cinefantastique*, but the film didn't come to fruition. Story has it that a studio exec rejected the project but still billed them as if it had been greenlit, absconding with the upfront funds.

Living with his then-wife Penny in 1982, Tom purchased at a film convention to show off some of his art, including his designs for *The Cry of Cthulhu*. Lynn Willis, who worked for role-playing publisher Chaosium, brought him aboard.

"I worked for Chaosium for 18 years. Lynn Willis and Charlie Krank, who wrote a lot of the stories, would send me usually a Xerox paper with part of a description from a Lovecraft story. Sometimes, the description was so detailed that it was laid out like a medical examiner's report—you know, with the length and the weight, the colors and the textures. All that stuff. As close to a scientific explanation of the appendage, the pseudopod, or whatever it is. Then there's the other ones that, 'Should I try to describe the blasphemy before me, I would go insane.' *Draw one of those, Tom!* [*Laughs*] I just did the best I could with what I had. I got one wrong. I think it was called an Elder Being. It was a sort of squat, like an extended pumpkin. It had these radiating things out—the description was "like a comb." I thought, *OK, like a pocket comb*, so I gave it these bony protrusions, like wings. But then a fan wrote in and said, 'Actually, it was like a Roman comb, like a clamshell with

Copyright (C) 2020 Tom Sullivan. All Rights Reserved.

bristles.' So, it would radiate out rather than wing. So, I didn't get that one right, but I am told that my designs have been really influential, so I'm proud of that."

Does he have any favorites? "There's one called the Wendigo—this big, tall, lanky gray thing looming over a snowy landscape. And the Shoggoth I like a lot—the big blubbery mass of eyes and pseudopods and things. And this thing, I can't recall what it was [*resident expert Bill Adcock says it's a Dimensional Shambler*]—this big, tall, colorful thing that's actually pretty dumb. He's holding up his hand and admiring the shadow on the floor, but he might not be making the connection that it's him creating the shadow. It's dumb but a big, powerful

Copyright (C) 2020 Tom Sullivan. All Rights Reserved.

thing, and you wouldn't want to piss it off. I gave my book [S. Petersen's Field Guide to Cthulhu Monsters] that those were in to Frank Frazetta. He looked at it and said, 'I can't do what you do. You're just making things out of shapes and stuff. This one here looks like a mushroom from the corner of one of your paintings that you've just turned into a centerpiece.'"

When it came to continuing in the pro-effects world, Tom quickly concluded that the Hollywood way of working didn't suit him. "*Evil Dead II* wasn't a great experience. My depression had really kicked in, and my marriage was falling apart. I was faced with this terrible decision: Should I go on with my career, or should I stay with my wife? I'm sure that either decision would have been the wrong one. But I did go to California and did work on Chris Walas's *The Fly II*, which turned into factory work. All those really invigorating folks, really talented—but I was kind of the old guy at 32 or 33. One guy walked up to me and said, 'Nose hair!' Good, yep, you found one. He was also fairly rude to the women working in the lab. So, no, that wasn't for me."

In 1987, Penny died, and in 1992, Tom was involved in a serious car accident that left him with crippling depression. When he needed a friend the most, he found one in Pat Reese. "I knew Pat Reese when he was a kid, and he worked on *Within the Woods* with us. Then, I moved out to California for a couple of years. When I came back, that's when I had my car accident, in '92. And then we remet after that. We were just two depressed guys in a bar, so we started hanging out. He had VHS and a big screen TV. Forty-eight inches then was gigantic. So, we started having our Friday night movies at his place."

As Tom found himself a draw at horror cons, his *Evil Dead* museum grew, and Reese came aboard to create handsome and official *Necronomicon: Book of the Dead* replicas for sale. "He wanted to take a crack at it. And I was happy to let him. That wasn't something I would look forward to. And he took to it and turned it into a really special part of the product. All I had to do was print the pages. He bound them together in a really complex way, with cloth between the pages, so that even if the paper breaks, the book still holds up. And we've never had a complaint about a single one of them. What he did was really great."

Because horror fans are some of the easier-going folks around, Sullivan and Reese were quickly adopted by various con families across the world. ("I met Bernie Wrightson's son, John, and he's in special effects now because of the work I did on *Evil Dead*. That was cool!") Speaking only for Wastelanders, the show wouldn't be the same without Sullivan and Reese. Though the future of con-going is uncertain and the nature of chasing unlicensed artwork has become an endless and thankless task (If you see "Book of the Dead" merchandise offered, there is a good chance it is an unauthorized use of Tom's designs), during quieter moments, Tom is grateful when looking back at his place in film history.

"I never won the lotto because I worked on *Evil Dead*. I wish there were more cash attached to it, but… you know. I had full faith in Sam. He was a walking encyclopedia of film technique. He had a way of talking about film that broke down how they did it, right down to the editing beats that create things in peoples' minds without actually being there—through camera angles and sound and lighting and editing—to get things across. He knew how to get the most bang for the buck for whatever that's worth, and with him, it goes a long, long way. I'm really happy to have been a part of that."

PHOTO: Top row L/R: Ellen Sandweiss, Don Campbell, Taylor Moore, Bruce Campbell, Josh Becker, Dave Horton, Hal Delrich, Sam Raimi, Frank Holt, Betsy Baker, Tom Sullivan, Theresa Tilly, John Mason, Tim, & Rob.
Bottom row L/R: Janice Brock Holt, Jim Brock, Helen Brock, Vicky Brock Moore
(Photo taken by Chuck Hale, Citizen Tribune 1979. All Rights Reserved.)

"IS THIS AN AD OR AN ARTICLE?" DEPARTMENT: TOM SULLIVAN IN SPLATTER MOVIE: THE DIRECTOR'S CUT

Between the late '90s and mid-2000s, being an independent filmmaker wasn't that ludicrous an idea. The home video market was collapsing, but numerous smaller distributors were thriving by offering indie products. Don Dohler's formula of "blood, boobs, and beasts" gave creative filmmakers a lot of leeway in the stories they could tell. If you could figure out how to make *Ordinary People* with two kills and a lesbian scene, you could likely find an outfit willing to gamble 1,000 units on your masterpiece, and FYE and Sam Goody would slap it on their shelves between *Daddy Day Care* and *Cannibal Holocaust*.

It was also an extremely self-aware time. The newly minted indie gods, Quentin Tarantino and Kevin Smith, gave us permission to crawl up our own asses—sorry, explore our favorite genres via deconstruction and self-absorption. Wes Craven and Kevin Williamson did more than dip a toe into this particular lake, and *Scream* reinvigorated the horror movie genre, which, up until that point, was still decried by the mainstream critics as a cross between porn and misogyny instruction manuals. The box office responded, and there was a demand again for horror.

The slasher film was particularly attractive from a budgetary standpoint, came with a ready-made formula, and could be applied to any situation, from slumber parties to Tupperware parties (wherever lesbians and murderers would be likely found). And while we'd already attempted a skewering parody of slashers with *Severe Injuries*, we at Happy Cloud Pictures found there were still deep waters to plumb.

After a couple of rounds with Carol J. Clover's *Men, Women, and Chainsaws*, Amy Lynn Best and I managed to hack out a pretty decent deconstruction of both the slasher movie and the horror industry, tackling feminism, sexism, and how the two exist within the genre and the business. We wrapped it in the mockumentary style in order to take advantage of the loose production value and narrative compression (which also led itself to some nifty surreal sequences).

I'm lying. We had access to the Hundred Acres Manor haunted

attraction in South Park, Pa, and by "access," I mean "full run of the place." We wrote the script in about a week so that we could shoot throughout the summer while the haunt was in construction. We couldn't control the environment, so we had to incorporate the construction into the narrative. The decision to go meta was the best solution. The idea to make it a story about filmmakers making a movie about filmmakers making a movie— and cleverly calling the central film *Tesseract*—was too tempting to resist.[1] I also liked the idea of the killer dressed as the film-in-the-film's murderer, wearing the same rubber mask (designed by Don Bumgarner). It provided the opportunity for a lot of red herrings (e.g., Who is really in the mask?), which we didn't quite take advantage of.

It was a priceless opportunity to make a too-clever gore film with our friends, with a ready-made location offering dozens of decorated sets and, this time, us not using all of our own money (thanks to a couple of generous investors). This enabled us to think out of the box when it came to casting. This brings me to the title of the piece.

We thought having Tom Sullivan in the film as himself would be a load of fun. A longtime friend of ours thanks to Cinema Wasteland, Tom and his partner, Pat Reese, had provided us with official and lovingly made Necronomicons for our films in the past and had always supported us. Tom is a big, loveable guy, and his big lovability provided us with the

ending of the film. Since the story was so chiral, I didn't know how to bring the silly thing full circle. Tom signing on solved that problem for me.

When I look back at the history of our films, *Splatter Movie* is my favorite production because of how collaborative it was. Under Amy's direction, we had a dozen different camera people running around and composing their own strange and surreal scenes. Since the majority of the haunt was already pre-set and lit, we had little to do in terms of hauling equipment. And since it involved a film-in-a-film, it didn't matter if lights got in the shot. If a sound blew a take, we could call attention to it and make it a scene-in-a-scene. Mistakes literally worked within the concept, which made a lot of what we did very stress-free. It was like running around in a low-tech Disneyland for eight weeks.

Again, Tom was a big part of that. Having more cred than the rest of us, our effects people especially came in as Tom's fans and left as his friends. He did some makeup as well, first on

---

1   But to quote Shirley in *Community*, "Come on, Charlie Kaufman, some of us have to go to work in the morning."

61

his nephew, Sean Riordan (who came along to fulfill Tom's "Best Uncle Ever" bingo square), and then on Amy for the framing device. He ad-libbed with the best of us and came up with a couple of the intentionally awkward "this is who I am" interview scenes.

If you haven't watched *Splatter Movie*, you're not alone, but **I'm about to destroy the ending**.

We asked Tom to be in it at first just to have a celebrity cameo. But it hit us as we pitched him: "How would you like to play yourself in a horror movie...wait, how would you like to play yourself *as the villain*?"

This is Tom Sullivan, the man who created the Book of the Dead, its Kandarian dagger, the body meltdown in *Evil Dead*, and one of the nicest guys you'd ever meet. He decided to go method on our set and start killing off our stars and extras. The matter-of-fact, down-home way he monologues at the end is both terrifying and hysterical. And that's what gave us our movie, because Tom is our friend and I used to have my doubts that he was capable of murder.

I kid.

The thing that I most take away from that summer is that Tom was willing to drive from Michigan to Pittsburgh to come play with us. While we'd proven ourselves to be more or less professional in the past, Tom took the risk that he'd have a great time. He gambled that he'd have a place to sleep that wasn't just one of our couches and that we'd feed him sufficiently to keep him alive for a couple of days. And if you think I'm joking, you've never yourself experienced the Wild West of indie filmmaking. We didn't have TikTok or Instagram for spur-of-the-moment filmmaking. Ineptitude took planning.

But Tom rolled the dice and joined in the game. That summer, we were all Lost Boys in Neverland, all armed with cameras and fake blood. When you ask me what I love about filmmaking, I think of Amy and me getting to run a studio and hang with all of our friends. And *Evil Dead*'s Tom Sullivan joining both.

Splatter Movie: The Director's Cut is available on DVD, along with a companion screenplay annotated by director Best and an intro by Tom Sullivan. Exclusively through www.happycloudpublishing.com

See? Told ya. Ad.

Director/star Amy Lynn Best with (?) as Grendel. Copyright Happy Cloud Pictures. All Rights Reserved.

IN THE MOUTH OF MADNESS: ONE OF JOHN CARPENTER'S BEST FILMS THAT NEVER GETS MENTIONED ALONGSIDE JOHN CARPENTER'S BEST FILMS

by Jason Lane

John Carpenter's *In the Mouth of Madness* did not do very well when it was released, and looking back, it probably shouldn't have. It followed none of the templates that then-recent horror films were following. It wasn't an example of A-to-B-to-C storytelling. Hell, even the protagonist wasn't the most likeable of people. I mean, who makes an insurance investigator the hero of a story? I remember watching when it came out on VHS (ask your folks, kids) with some friends who were very satisfied with what they had just watched, while the others' reactions were more among the lines of "What the hell was that?"

I immediately liked the movie. I thought it was smart, took risks, found a way to make a complex plot manageable enough for public consumption, had some legit creepy moments, and was littered with a ton of Easter eggs—and all of this besides the fact that it was a good horror movie. People forget the fact that it's just a good movie. Damn good acting, damn good special effects, damn good writing, damn good directing; that just adds up to a damn good movie. And yet it constantly gets ignored when great horror films are discussed and other Carpenter faves are mentioned repeatedly. Not that those films don't deserve their praises, but this one almost always is forgotten. So, why?

FROM BEYOND,
or 'Xactly Is This Movie About?

If you hate spoilers or haven't watched this movie yet, be warned because I'll be discussing key parts here. I'm going to try to generalize as much as possible, but I just want to let you know that I'm not going to slow down the entire class just so one student can catch up.

Also, I'm going to sometimes abbreviate *In the Mouth of Madness* as *ITMOM*, as I'm already tired as hell of writing out *In the Mouth of Madness*. Cool?

The film opens in a sanitarium where a new inmate is being brought in. Bits of news and gossip from the staff lets the audience in on the fact that what we're watching here is happening after some seriously freaky shit has gone down. The new patient (Sam Neill) is reallllly stressed. He's then visited by a doctor (David Warner) who's trying to figure out why the seriously freaky shit has gone down. Through flashback, the audience learns that the new patient's name is John Trent, and he is a rather unscrupulous insurance investigator who is at the end of helping a colleague (Bernie Casey) out with a large claims case. Over lunch, his friend drops a message that one of the biggest publishing agencies wants to hire him for a delicate case. While they're discussing this matter, a psychotic-looking man carrying an axe from across the street exits a bookstore, sees them both eating in the diner, calmly walks across the street, and shatters their nearby window. Jumping on their table and looking right at Trent, the crazed man asks him a question (that should have become a great tagline/catchphrase):

"Do you read Sutter Cane?"

Seriously? Don't you want to buy a shirt with that on it *right now*? Anyway, he raises the axe to kill Trent but is shot dead by the police before he can do so. Trent later meets with Arcane Publishing Company, the large publishing company his friend mentioned, and its director,

Sam Neill as John Trent. (All Photos this section copyright New Line Cinema. All Rights Reserved.)

Jackson Harglow (Charlton Heston). Harglow wants to hire Trent because their best-selling author ever, Sutter Cane, has gone missing right when he was supposed to turn in his final book, which is called (wait for it) *In the Mouth of Madness*. The publishing company wants to know if Cane is still alive, dead, at Denny's, or finishing his book. Cane's editor, Linda Styles (Julie Carmen), lays out Cane's publishing history with his books being published in all countries and languages over the world, outselling "the Bible and Stephen King's works" combined. Harglow also mentions that there are extreme cases of mental trauma and violence with some of Cane's "less stable readers."

Trent takes the case but is convinced that it's outright bullcrap, even when learning that Cane's agent was the man who axe-attacked him. Styles gives him a selection of Cane's books, hoping that reading them will give him a clue as to the author's whereabouts. Reading them gives Trent severe nightmares, but also a way to figure out Cane's whereabouts using a rendered map made of those very same book covers. The map points Trent and Styles to an unnamed town in New Hampshire. They find the town, check into the local hotel, and learn that Cane is there and the town's gone to hell from the moment he arrived.

Varying escalating factors of unease and madness meet the them both. Finally, they come face to face with Cane (Jürgen Prochnow). Cane tells Trent a multitude of items, with the most important ones listed below:
- There was an ancient race of monstrous gods that lived in this universe before it was here. Now they're coming back.
- Cane's writings/books are a bridge from that monstrous world to this one as it slowly overwrites our reality.
- The final book, *In the Mouth of Madness*, will be the end of humanity.
- Trent learns that he is merely a character created by Cane.

Cane's plan is for Trent to bring the manuscript back to Arcane Publishing so that the world will start to destroy itself. Trent manages to escape Cane, the monsters, and that crazy town. He finds himself in a field back in the "real" world, with Styles missing. He also finds that he has a copy of Cane's manuscript, which he destroys immediately. He eventually gets back to New York and Arcane Publishing, where he tells Harglow his entire story, which confuses the hell out of the director. Harglow says that he never sent a Linda Styles with Trent and doesn't know who she is. In the other matter, Harglow says that Trent arrived there months earlier and gave him the manuscript back then. *ITMOM* had been on sale in stores all that time and was even being made into a movie.

Trent, unsure of what is real and what is not, wanders the city and witnesses an even larger escalation of paranoia and violence. Going by the diner where he was attacked at the beginning of the movie, he finds a customer exiting the bookstore who has obviously been affected by Cane's writing. He asks the reader, "Do you read Sutter Cane?" and kills him with an axe similarly to how the agent was going to kill him earlier. Trent is then arrested and placed in the asylum seen at the beginning of the film. The person interviewing him tells him that not only is Cane's *ITMOM* selling like crazy, but they've made a movie version that is premiering worldwide.

Flash-forward to the aftermath of the movie premiere. Trent finds his way out of the asylum and wanders through the chaos-ravaged streets. He makes his way to a movie theater where *ITMOM* is playing. He sits to watch it and sees everything from his life playing out on the screen in the exact way he saw it, confirming that he is a character created by Cane merely to bring the manuscript to the world. The last shot is him laughing hysterically while the world falls further into decay.

Lots to unpack here.

First off, there's a whole lotta story crammed into a mere 95 minutes. Not afraid of being intelligent to the point of losing a casual viewer gives the movie more bite than most, especially when it starts throwing the entire concept of reality into question. Carpenter voiced the matter of quantum physics in his prior work *Prince of Darkness*, but he leaves out any scientific explanations in *In the Mouth of Madness*. Here, it's merely another reality taking a foothold in this one and growing through the belief of the populace.

This movie is the third of Carpenter's Apocalypse Trilogy, the other two being *The Thing* and *Prince of Darkness*. In these films, the threat is capable/likely/damn well gonna kill all life on the planet. Whereas *The Thing* was a deeply layered testament to equal parts horror and paranoia and *Prince of Darkness* was an Italian horror-laced homage to the war between faith and science versus a threat more powerful than both, *In the Mouth of Madness* does one better by including an overriding deus ex machina.

Example: The movie *Halloween* has a scene where Laurie Strode (Jamie Lee Curtis) stabs masked killer Michael Myers and then, thinking he's dead, drops the knife she was using. The viewer asks, "Why the hell would you drop that?" If it were *In the Mouth of Madness*, the answer would be simple: She dropped the knife because Sutter Cane wrote her doing that. And unlike the other Apocalypse Trilogy films, where the endings are ambiguous, this one leaves the viewer with several questions. The lead one is wondering whether John Trent was originally a Sutter Cane creation or is one now since Cane wrote it that way.

Added to this are the small details, such as spending a chunk of the budget on a legion of grotesque monsters only to show them in glimpses and shadow, or the H.P. Lovecraft homages littered heavily throughout the entire film, or the visual tapestry foreshadowing the importance of the book covers with them used as advertising wallpaper/posters on street buildings.

It's certainly a film that you have to pay attention to.

IMPORTANT INFO,
or Take a Look!

I had forgotten exactly what a boom year it was for movies in 1995. As far as big-budget or high-end cinema, there were plenty of choices, with *Braveheart* (try not to yell "Freedom!"), *The American President*, *Casino*, *The Usual Suspects*, and *Apollo 13*. Family films were represented well with the huge hits like *Pocahontas*, *Jumanji*, *Babe*, and some little-remembered film called *Toy Story*. Comic book fans didn't have the quality selection they had the year before but were fairly happy with *Batman Forever*, *Ghost in the Shell*, *Judge Dredd*, future cult favorite *Tank Girl*, and *Tales from the Crypt: Demon Knight*. Action fans had uber-hits *Die Hard with a Vengeance*, *Bad Boys*, *Heat*, *Rumble in the Bronx*, *Desperado*, and the franchise re-invigorating *Goldeneye* to satisfy them. Comedy fans had *Clueless*, *Friday*, *Mallrats*, (my guilty pleasure) *Houseguest*, *The Brady Bunch Movie*, and, of course, the subtle and sublime genius of *Ace Ventura: When Nature Calls*. Horror/fantasy/sci-fi had a decent selection of films with *Lord of Illusions*, *Candyman: Farewell to the Flesh*, *Copycat*, *Congo*, *12 Monkeys*, *Village of the Damned*, *Species*, *The Prophecy*, *Dolores Claiborne*, the dual daikaiju romps *Gamera: Guardian of the Universe* and *Godzilla vs. Destroyah*, and the David Fincher classic *Se7en*. There were cult films aplenty with the cheesy-yet-satisfying *The Quick and the Dead*; *Empire Records*; *To Wong Foo, Thanks for Everything! Julie Newmar*; *Four Rooms*; the incredibly depressing as hell *Kids*; *Jeffery*; *The Basketball Diaries*; *Swimming with Sharks*; and the instant contender for either the worst-best movie ever or the best-worst movie ever, *Showgirls*.

A lot of the money that went into Hollywood productions transferred over the years to shows like *The Sopranos*, *Lost*, *The Shield*, *Deadwood*, *The Wire*, *The West Wing*, *The X-Files*, *Six Feet Under*, and *24*, with the budgets for those shows easily equaling anything made for cinema.

So, why did I mention all of this fascinating yet useless information? Movies relied on making up any type of back end in the home market (video and post-cinema sales mostly). So, while an overly smart, ambitious film like *In the Mouth of Madness* may not have done great at the box office, it would surely do well after.

Except it *didn't* do too well, probably due to the glut of quality movies mentioned above. Copies probably weren't ordered in excess for rental either. If you were a business owner, would you rather have three copies of a movie that you're not sure will make back its costs or 15 copies of *Ace Ventura: When Nature Calls*? And Carpenter didn't even take long to work on this film. He worked on the admittedly disappointing *Memoirs of an Invisible Man* in '92, *Body Bags* in '93, started work on *In the Mouth of Madness* in '94, and then immediately started work on *Village of the Damned* in '95, followed by *Escape from L.A.* in '96. Hard to fault a working man, but at this stage, Carpenter was working one film to the next. By the time the full results came in on *In the Mouth of Madness*, Carpenter was already knee-deep in other projects.

WHO GOES THERE?
or Who Is in This Movie?

In the Mouth of Madness is similar to Carpenter's other works in that it's

loaded with great character actors. He also keeps up his tradition of working with the same recurring actors. The following is a list of the main actors from this film, other films they're associated with, and my two cents' worth.

Sam Neill as John Trent: He got the attention of horror fans playing a grown-up Damien in *Omen III: The Final Conflict* and starring in the disturbing-as-hell Andrzej Żuławski film *Possession* before getting famous-as-hell in *Jurassic Park*. He's played dozens of roles (Make sure to check out *Hunt for the Wilderpeople*), but he's still never shied away from his horror roots, playing in the awesomely morbid *Event Horizon*.

Julie Carmen as Linda Styles: Carmen gained worldwide notice in 1980's *Gloria*. She garnered favorable reviews in *The Milagro Beanfield War* but got my attention as the alluring Regine Dandridge in *Fright Night Part 2*. Side note: She's crazy smart as well, pursuing academics all the while to where she's a licensed/practicing psychotherapist and a certified/licensed yoga therapist. Yeah, what have you done with your life?

David Warner as Dr. Wrenn: Warner is an established veteran actor who attended the Royal Academy of Dramatic Art. There's not enough time or space to even begin to mention his accomplishments, so here's just some of my personal faves. Horror fans would recognize him from *The Omen*, although he had no problem playing someone evil (Jack the Ripper) in *Time After Time*. He actually played someone named Evil in the wonderfully dark *Time Bandits*. Sci-fi fans were well-represented by Warner when he played both villains (Ed Dillinger/Sark) in *Tron*, the peace-attempting Klingon Chancellor Gorkon in *Star Trek: The Undiscovered Country*, and the universally hated Cardassian Gul Madred, who tortured the ever-loving shit out of Captain Picard in *Star Trek: The Next Generation* (I forget, were there four or five lights?). He was also the voice of Ra's al Ghul on *Batman: The Animated Series*.

John Glover as the sadly not-seen-enough Dr. Saperstein: Glover played Mr. Clamp in *Gremlins 2: The*

New Batch, Bill Murray's network rival in *Scrooged*, and the scene-stealing Lionel Luthor on *Smallville*, but I'll always appreciate him for playing a disturbingly optimistic life salesman in the dark, dark, dark comedy *Ed and His Dead Mother*. He was also the voice of the Riddler on *Batman: The Animated Series.*

Jürgen Prochnow as Sutter Cane: Prochnow found stardom overseas with *Das Boot*, which led to international roles in *Dune*, *Beverly Hills Cop II*, *Twin Peaks: Fire Walk with Me*, and the awesomely awful 1995 *Judge Dredd*. But as far as favorites, I'm going to go with Baron Wolfgang von Wolfhausen from Broken Lizard's *Beerfest*, the only character that can possibly hang with Max von Sydow's Brewmeister Smith from *Strange Brew*. Sadly, Prochnow played no role whatsoever in *Batman: The Animated Series.*

Bernie Casey as Robinson, Trent's diner buddy: Casey played the gargoyle leader in *Gargoyles* but came into his own with parts in *Cleopatra Jones* and *I'm Gonna Git You Sucka*, as well as playing the eternally frustrated San Dimas High history teacher Mr. Ryan in *Bill and Ted's Excellent Adventure*. He also played Lambda Lambda fraternity head U.N. Jefferson in *Revenge of the Nerds* and is the only cast member to have aged well over the years. Also, he did not lend his voice to *Batman: The Animated Series*. Wait a minute—Casey *did* play in *Batman Beyond*. Does that count?

Charlton Heston as Jackson Harglow: Dear god, if you think I'm going to try to encapsulate any of this man's career, you are crazy. I'll just say he played iconic roles in *Planet of the Apes*, *Ben-Hur*, *Touch of Evil* (in which he was made up to look Latino instead of the white, white guy he is), and the both compelling yet dull *Soylent Green*.

Peter Jason as Mr. Paul: Jason has over 260 acting roles to his credit, to the point where his filmography has its own Wikipedia™ page. Goddamn! Also, at seven films, he may hold the record for the most appearances in John Carpenter movies. And you know damn well that he played on *Batman: The Animated Series*. As MANY!

Hayden Christensen also played a bit part. The future sand-hating, youngling-chopping, Jedi-betraying Anakin Skywalker got his start here playing a paperboy who wanders across a just-escaped-from-crazy-town Sam Neill. Although he is known worldwide for his groundbreaking work in *Star Wars: Episode II - Attack of the Clones* and *Star Wars: Episode III - Revenge of the Sith*, if you want to see a little range from Christensen, check out his performances in *The Virgin Suicides* and *Shattered Glass*, where he won a ton of critical praise. No, seriously! But, sadly enough, he did not work on *Batman: The Animated Series.*

CRITICAL REVIEW,
or Why Don't We Just Wait Here for a Little While...See What Happens

Reviews were mixed at the time when *In the Mouth of Madness* was released, with most people saying it was either kinda good or kinda lame, but like a lot of Carpenter's works, it's gained more favor over the years. More often than not, the negative reviews given at the time seem to be reasons to want to watch the film, with the words "complicated," "weird," "intriguing," and "overly ambitious" used repeatedly. Those words just so happen to draw my interest, but hey, maybe it's just me. I also know that the more people learn about H.P. Lovecraft (Spoiler: He was crazy racist), the more people might tune this film out without evening viewing it. This is probably the same way that *Harry Potter* fans are feeling right now being all-inclusive as anything and hearing J.K. Rowling give some *opinions* on transgendered individuals. What can you do?

As with many of Carpenter's films, *In the Mouth of Madness* would have done much better if it had been released today, as I've noticed filmmakers now trying to catch up with works Carpenter did three or four decades earlier. *In the Mouth of Madness* is like its Apocalypse Trilogy brethren: an unappreciated overachiever in quality that underachieved with the public. The nice thing about now is that it's still being discovered by new fans who are appreciating it for what it is: a masterpiece of horror cinema that, if undeserving of being mentioned among the greats, at least deserves being mentioned.

Seriously, though, if I mention John Carpenter and someone says *Ghosts of Mars* before *In the Mouth of Madness*, I'm going to be on the news.

"Say, John, can I AXE you something?" (Ugh, no! Boo!)
(Bernie Casey, Conrad Bergschneider, Neill.)

STUART GORDON: MAESTRO OF MONSTERS
by Bill Adcock

Photo copyright Stuart Gordon. All Rights Reserved.

The creations of H.P. Lovecraft have experienced a renaissance over the past 40 years. The visage of the half-octopus, half-dragon god-monster Cthulhu can be found on T-shirts, buttons, Funko Pops, and more. Personally, I feel that Stuart Gordon is half responsible for that renaissance (I credit the other half to Sandy Petersen and the *Call of Cthulhu* roleplaying game, but that's outside the scope of this piece). Gordon's wild, gore-drenched modernizations of some of Lovecraft's iconic tales brought new attention to the author and triggered a critical reevaluation of Lovecraft's work. But how much of what Gordon brought to the screen was faithful to Lovecraft's vision, and how much of it was his own? To answer that, we have to look at Gordon's Lovecraftian filmography.

Our story begins with 1985's *Re-Animator*, Gordon's film based on the first half of Lovecraft's ghoulishly comedic "Herbert West—Reanimator." Lovecraft never cared much for the story himself, but he'd been offered $5 a chapter to write something for a periodical called *Home Brew*, and that was a lot of money for a freelancer in 1921. The story he turned in was intended as a parody of Mary Shelley's *Frankenstein* and represents one of the earliest instances of zombies brought to life as mindless gut-munchers by science.

Gordon took the central premise, updated it to the 1980s, and cranked the grotesque horror-comedy aspect up to about 13. Working with special effects technician John Naulin and a folder full of morgue photos, Gordon brought to uncanny cinematic life some of the most gruesome and realistic corpses ever to shamble onto the silver screen. Purportedly, 24 gallons of stage blood were thrown around over the course of filming, especially once the zombies begin to explode from overdosing on West's reanimation serum. Lovecraft was notably averse to including women in his stories, necessitating Gordon, producer Brian Yuzna, and screenwriter Dennis Paoli to add a love interest.

Gaunt, pale Jeffrey Combs is perfectly cast as the narcissistic, amoral West, contrasted by leading-man-material Bruce Abbott in the role of Dan Cain, West's roommate and the unnamed narrator of the story. Barbara Crampton appears as Cain's love interest, Megan Halsey, and David Gale plays Carl Hill, the villainous doctor eager to steal West's research. A scene between Gale and Crampton late in the film, in which the decapitated-but-reanimated Dr. Hill attempts to rape Megan, allegedly resulted in Gale's wife divorcing him, or so the rumors go. Needless to say, it wasn't a scene that appeared in Lovecraft's story, and the old gent from Providence doubtlessly would have had an apoplectic fit if he'd lived to see it.

Re-Animator proved to be a success and was quickly followed by another adaptation, 1986's *From Beyond*, again scripted by Paoli and produced by Yuzna. Lovecraft's original story was a fairly staid affair, involving an unnamed narrator explaining to police the death of scientist Crawford Tillinghast as the result of his efforts to peer into a parallel dimension. The story is only a few pages long, and Gordon, Yuzna, and Paoli had to add a great deal to get a full-length film out of Lovecraft's story.

Under Gordon's direction, *From Beyond* became a neon-drenched exercise in creature effects and sexuality. Dr. Crawford Tillinghast (Combs again) has been relegated to serving as the laboratory assistant to a Dr. Edward Pretorius (Ted Sorel), whose experiments into pineal gland stimulation have grown out of his taste for BDSM. Regular kink having become too vanilla for him, Pretorius is looking for new avenues of pleasure using a device called the Resonator, which bathes its surroundings in purple light. When an extradimensional monster bites off Pretorius's head, Tillinghast is taken to an insane asylum. Convinced of his sincerity, psychiatrist Katherine McMichaels (Crampton again) and detective Bubba Brown (genre mainstay Ken Foree) break Tillinghast out to recreate the experiment. Soon, a mutating, brain-eating Pretorius is on the loose, McMichaels is dolled up in leather fetish gear, and Tillinghast's pineal gland is sticking out of his forehead on a stalk. Oops!

About the only things the film *From Beyond* has in common with the source story (which is, admittedly, like, five pages long) are a guy named Tillinghast and a machine that makes parallel worlds visible to each other. Gordon and his team filled the gaps with more neon-drenched erotic mayhem than Lovecraft's puritanical heart would have been able to take, and they pulled off a very entertaining sci-fi horror film. It pairs nicely for a double feature with the following year's *Hellraiser*, but I digress.

Naulin, along with Greg Nicotero and John Carl Buechler, worked on creature effects for *From Beyond*, and the results are spectacular. The shambling, devolving Pretorius, less human with each appearance, deserves a place alongside Brundlefly and Pinhead as an iconic monster of the 1980s. Stealing every scene, though, are the composited, glowing horrors of the other dimension, jellyfish- and eel-like creatures that swirl and swim through the air before attacking. The electric purple glow of the Resonator, the color so saturated as to be almost painful to look at, really highlights the alienness of this other world and its corrupting effects on the humans who encounter it.

If 1986's *From Beyond* bore little resemblance to its source material, 1995's *Castle Freak* is almost unrecognizable as a Lovecraft adaptation. Loosely inspired by Lovecraft's early Poe-influenced short story "The Outsider," *Castle Freak* is a surprisingly smart and sophisticated film considering its release under the Full Moon label of Charles Band.

Reuniting Combs and Crampton as John and Susan Reilly, *Castle Freak* tells the story of the Reilly family dealing with two upheavals; first, John's drunk driving cost their daughter, Rebecca (Jessica Dollarhide), her sight in a car crash, and second, the family has inherited a castle in Italy. Hoping a change of scenery will help mend their strained family, the Reillys soon begin to experience strange noises, broken items, and Rebecca insisting she's been getting a mute nocturnal visitor. It's soon apparent that not only do the Reillys have company in the castle, but that it's family and its name is Giorgio.

While the theme of long-hidden family secrets rising up to threaten the modern day is a favorite of Lovecraft's and is indeed one that appears in "The Outsider," *Castle Freak* is a very different story. "The Outsider" is about a long-dead corpse that reanimates and leaves the crypt to crash a dinner party its descendants are throwing. The only similarity between the two stories is a sequence in which the monster recognizes himself as a monster by seeing his reflection in a mirror and reaching out to touch it.

While the Lovecraft connection may be tenuous, I'm more than happy to highlight it here, as I consider *Castle Freak* an underseen gem. The gore is unrelentingly savage, including a few things I can't recall seeing in another film and don't wish to spoil for you here, while the full-body prosthetics used to bring Giorgio to life (only the second movie to use full-body prosthetics instead of a suit) are effectively grotesque. More than that, though, the storytelling is better than you might expect. The Reillys' deteriorating family situation, even before Giorgio gets loose, is handled with a light touch and so doesn't descend into parody. A stand-out sequence features Rebecca learning Italian via books on tape and weeping as every example sentence is visual (e.g., "The sky is blue").

Gordon followed up the tenuous Lovecraft connection of *Castle Freak* with his most faithful adaptation since *Re-Animator*, 2001's *Dagon*, adapting the novella *The Shadow over Innsmouth*. The film follows American Paul Marsh (Ezra Godden, as Combs was, at this point, a little past playing twentysomethings) and his girlfriend, Bárbara (Raquel Meroño), after a boating accident off the coast of Spain leaves them stranded in the decaying fishing village of Imboca (a pun; *boca* is Spanish for "mouth"). Soon, however, Bárbara has disappeared and the unnerving behavior of the locals has Paul running for his life through the darkened streets. Only the aged and drunken fisherman Ezequiel knows what's going on and can fill Paul in on the sacrifices the town has made for prosperity—and will be making again tonight....

I have no other word to describe this film except sumptuous. I genuinely believe that this is the best adaptation of *The Shadow over Innsmouth* that I could, in good conscience, ask for. Filmed in Combarro, Spain—a Galician fishing village famous for its "old town," which dates back to the 1700s—every shot conveys Imboca as a town whose past sins dominate its present existence. The locals are grotesque and varied, with no two people having quite the same mutations. Webbed hands, needle-like teeth, and bulging, staring eyes are common and realized beautifully through prosthetics, and when you get to some of the more advanced or unusual inhabitants...when Macarena Gómez, playing the priestess Uxia, throws back the comforter, revealing that she has a pair of 10-foot-long tentacles instead of legs, the combination of puppetry and prosthetics really sells the illusion.

The gore, likewise, is what we've come to expect from a Stuart Gordon horror film; faces are sliced off, limbs are torn off, and the audience is even treated to an attempted self-immolation sequence. There's a little bit of CGI toward the end, but overall, it doesn't detract from what a practical effects-lover's dream the overall film is.

Other than moving the setting of the film from a decrepit New England fishing village to a decrepit Galician fishing village, the biggest change made is the introduction of Bárbara, the love interest. I can excuse it, given how rarely (and poorly, when he did) Lovecraft wrote relationships; and realistically, Bárbara is here as a plot device to keep Paul in town instead of sensibly fleeing for his life and to show her tits in the final act. They're a nice pair, don't get me wrong, but I don't really feel like Meroño was given much to work with in the script, and I feel like Bárbara could have easily been left out.

And now, at last, we come to Gordon's final Lovecraft adaptation, 2005's hour-long "Dreams in the Witch House," part of the *Masters of Horror* anthology series produced by Anchor Bay. Godden returns as Walter Gilman,

a mathematics student just looking for a quiet apartment to rent to work on his thesis. The only place in his price range turns out to be an attic apartment in a building dating back to the 1700s. He's got one neighbor who prays loudly all night and another whose infant has been bedeviled by a persistent and bloodthirsty rat.

Before long, Gilman discovers that his attic room was once the home of Keziah Mason, a reputed witch and child murderer, along with her familiar, a rat-like beast called Brown Jenkin. As Mason begins to figure more and more prominently into his dreams, Gilman finds himself losing control over his waking life as well.

I'm not as big a fan of this one as I am of the other four films I've discussed. I'm not sure if it's just that the film

75

feels a little rushed to fit its available running time or what. There's some decent gore (including a sequence of Mason clawing a pentagram into Gilman's back while having sex with him) and an appreciated reliance on practical effects—though some viewers might get a chuckle out of the forced-perspective shots used to realize Brown Jenkin. Overall, the film falls a little flat to me and lacks some of the rewatchability of earlier films. This isn't to say it's bad or poor work on Gordon's part by any means. Other than introducing a single-mother love interest for Gilman and bloodying the whole film up, "Dreams in the Witch House" is very faithful to the original narrative, though it unfortunately lacks some of the more hallucinatory visuals Lovecraft described in his prose. I would definitely have liked to have seen some of the unearthly realms Mason leads Gilman through in his dreams, but unfortunately, it was not to be this time around—again, see that hour-long run-time.

Stuart Gordon did more than almost anyone else to return Lovecraft's body of work to the public eye, and films like *Re-Animator* and *From Beyond* helped pave the way for our current world, in which Cthulhu is almost a household name. While the films weren't always particularly letter-accurate to Lovecraft's stories, they were frequently faithful in the broad strokes, acting as visual love letters to Lovecraft's feverish imagination but still presenting the Grand Guignol stylings that horror fans in the 1980s had come to expect. Gordon's passing is a huge blow to the world of horror cinema, on par with the loss of Romero or Fulci.

Macarena Gómez as Uxía Cambarro is Gordon's Dagon.
(Copyright Filmax International/Lions Gate Entertainment. All Rights Reserved.)

STUART GORDON: ARTAUD FOR ARTAUD'S SAKE

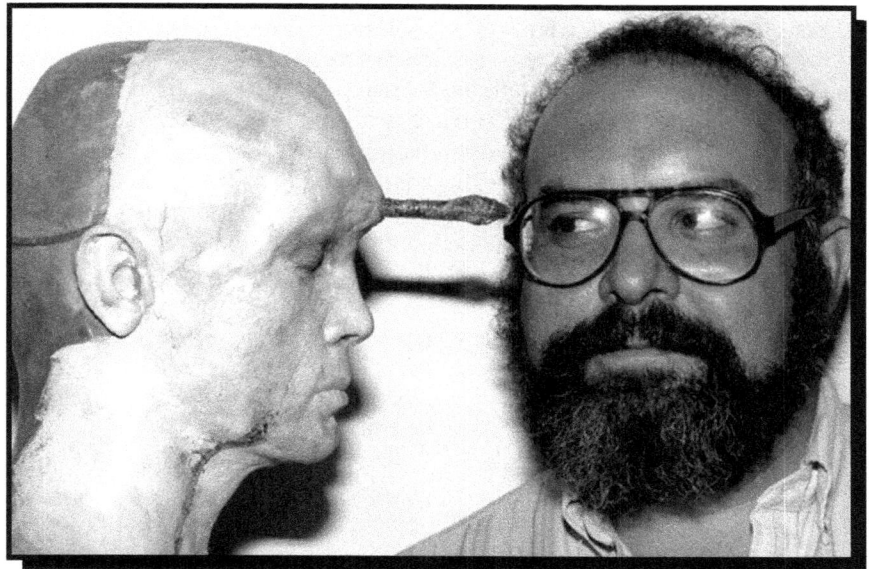

Stuart Gordon and Jeffrey Combs' Tillinghast mask. (Photographer unknown. All Rights Reserved.)

"One of the most influential theatre theorists of the 20th century and a key figure of the European avant-garde, Antonin Artaud (1896–1948) developed the ideas behind the Theatre of Cruelty [...] both a philosophy and a discipline. Artaud wanted to disrupt the relationship between audience and performer. The 'cruelty' in Artaud's thesis was sensory; it exists in the work's capacity to shock and confront the audience, to go beyond words and connect with the emotions: to wake up the nerves and the heart. He believed gesture and movement to be more powerful than text. Sound and lighting could also be used as tools of sensory disruption. The audience, he argued, should be placed at the centre of a piece of performance. Theatre should be an act of 'organised anarchy.'"[1]

When Stuart Gordon passed this year, I have to admit that I was surprised that two very distinct audiences mourned him. On one side was the horror fan camp, those who knew him almost exclusively for his gleefully subversive and gory horror movies—particularly his transformative Lovecraft adaptations *Re-Animator*, *From Beyond*, and *Dagon*. On the other side were the people who knew him for his foundational work in theatre, particularly in Chicago's landmark Organic Theater Company, which launched the careers of David Mamet (*Glengarry Glen Ross*), Dennis Franz

---

[1] Tripney, Natasha. "Antonin Artaud and the Theatre of Cruelty." *British Library*, 7 Sept. 2017, https://www.bl.uk/20th-century-literature/articles/antonin-artaud-and-the-theatre-of-cruelty

(*NYPD Blue*), and William H. Macy (*Fargo*). To someone on the outside looking in, you'd think both sides were talking about different men.

Truthfully, the man who so joyously filmed a severed head performing a sexual act/visual pun on a naked woman strapped to a gurney is the same man who mounted premiere performances of Ray Bradbury's *The Wonderful Ice Cream Suit* and Mamet's first play, *Sexual Perversity in Chicago*. Gordon was always about confrontational entertainment that subverted expectations. Just as you never knew what kind of movie you were going to get from Gordon— the anarchy of *Re-Animator*, the grim surrealism of *From Beyond*, the horrific dark comedy of *Stuck* and *Edmond*— the theatrical performances that he and wife, Carolyn Purdy-Gordon, mounted could be the assault of Artaud or the profound connectivity of *Bleacher Bums*.

One story I saw frequently recounted involved Gordon's production of *E/R*, a short-lived comedy-drama TV series set in a Chicago emergency room, directed by Gordon, conceived by Dr. Ronald Berman, produced by Norman Lear, and starring Elliot Gould. The factoid generally devolved into the "trivia" that a late addition to the cast, George Clooney, later earned his stardom on another medical series also called *ER*. While fun, this little paragraph that found its way into so many mainstream news aggregates fails to take into account the numerous

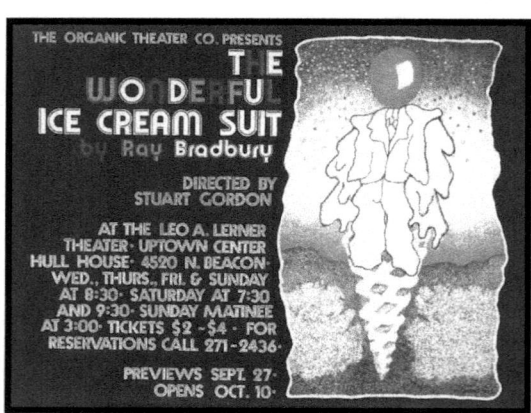

ballsy and bizarre performances from Gordon's past, beginning with his auspicious departure from the University of Wisconsin.

In 1968, Gordon and Purdy produced an adaptation of J.M. Barrie's seminal children's classic, *Peter Pan*, an often-misunderstood treatise of the cruelty of children. *Shooters and Chasers* author and then-cast member Lenny Kleinfeld recounted on his "Murder Is Everywhere" blog, "Stuart was doing a site-specific adaptation of the J.M. Barrie classic. Specifically, it embodied the sex, drugs, rock 'n' roll and political upheaval going down in Madison. Peaceful anti-war demonstrations on the campus had been attacked by the city police. Some of the students fought back, so what were essentially police riots were dubbed student riots. Several continued for days, ending only when the governor called out the National Guard to get between the cops and the students, not to mention get between the cops and the taxpayer-funded campus before they wrecked the place. Therefore, *Peter Pan* was now a free-spirited hippie dude. His sidekick, Tinkerbell, was a hairy guy in a fringed leather shirt who dealt acid—I mean, dispensed fairy dust, which sent Wendy and her brothers on a trip to Neverland, where the Lost Boys were a commune of semi-feral teens, the Indians were African-American Black Power radicals, and Captain Hook wasn't a pirate; he was a cop, as were his men, who wore leather jackets, helmets, and aviator shades. The trip Peter, Tink, Wendy, and her brothers took to Neverland consisted of a heavy-duty light show. The set and everyone on it was covered with deeply colored stage lights, pulsing oil projections, blacklights, strobes, and a movie of flowing lava, accompanied by 'In-A-Gadda-Da-Vida' played at brain-mulching volume. And, center stage, waiting to greet Peter and Wendy, was Stuart's Big Allegorical Move: six naked female dancers. They symbolized, he explained, innocence. Later, after the first dust-up between the Lost Boys and the cops, the women danced again—this time in tights, nude only from the waist up, to symbolize compromised innocence. Then, after Peter shoots and kills Hook—these were turbulent times, man—they symbolized the loss of innocence by dancing fully clothed, with fright wigs and monster makeup. Though, if I remember correctly, they wore leotards with no bras. As did a good portion of our audience. Ah, our audience. The previous semester, Stuart had done a fantastically creative, hilarious, and disturbing comedy that was a huge hit. So, when the 420 tickets for his *Peter Pan* were released—the Union gave them away free—they were gone in an hour."[2]

A photographer friend of Kleinfeld took some photos that wound up on the global wire service. According to Kleinfeld, "When we finished the matinee, we were greeted by reporters, cameras, and breaking news. Madison's district attorney had issued a statement: If we did our third and final performance, we'd be busted on indecent exposure charges. A recent Supreme Court decision had

---

2   Kleinfeld, Lenny. "Felony Nudity: Peter Pan." *Murder Is Everywhere*, Blogspot, 22 July 2013, https://murderiseverywhere.blogspot.com/2013/07/felony-nudity-peter-pan.html

rendered such laws unconstitutional in cases where the work had artistic and/or socially redeeming value. A prosecution would fail, or if it succeeded, would be overturned on appeal. But the D.A. was a republican who was up for reelection in a month. This was about political exposure, not nipple and genital exposure. And yet the university locked us out of the Play Circle so we couldn't do our final performance.

"So, we broke in. So, the school pulled the fuses. So, we lit some candles and occupied the theater. So, a deal was struck. If we left the theater, we'd be allowed to return and do a matinee for a tiny audience: the D.A., the chief of police, and three theater professors. After the show, the five would share their professional assessments of the play's socially redeeming allegorical nipples and genitals. In the meantime, the story surged way off the charts; Johnny Carson was cracking jokes about us on *The Tonight Show*."

Gordon and company were threatened by the D.A. and police chief. It was the D.A.'s opinion that the art was obscene. Parents forced their kids to drop out. The play was held at the student film society's room to sold-out performances, defying the law and the man, who had already issued arrest warrants for Gordon, Purdy, and another dancer (under a Jane Doe warrant; "They never caught her," said Kleinfeld). They saw the play through the run, and the D.A. won reelection. Gordon and Purdy decided that the university was an unsupportive and narrow institution.

Fleeing to Chicago, they founded the Organic Theater Company and proceeded to be even stranger for a while.

One notorious production was *The Game Show*, which sounds for all the world like the Stanford prison experiment on stage. As recounted by critic Linda Winer, *The Game Show* was dangerous art indeed.

"[With] Gordon's visceral, wildly original theatre productions, however, he was the force that first defined the untamable energy oversimplified later by the New York press as Steppenwolf's 'rock 'n' roll theatre.' In retrospect, I think Gordon and his Organic Theater Company were that, but they were at least as genetically linked to comic books, Grand Guignol hyper-realism, and Monster Roster, the post-war imagist movement in the visual arts."

Winer described *The Game Show* as "to this date, the scariest experience I ever had in the theatre. [...] At the door, seemingly at random, some of us were given ticket stubs with a mark, maybe an X, on them. By fluke, or perhaps nascent media savvy, I got an X. The structure was to be a live TV game show—itself an audacious idea back then—with contestants from the audience. Soon, the doors were locked (I remember chains) by ominous, muscular guards in uniforms. Before long, people were being beaten, stripped, bullied into submission, under the increasingly suspect assumption that surely it was only a show. When I was summoned to the stage, my theatre party began to worry. It was not that long since the '68 Convention, and it was increasingly a time when anything could happen. After all, they knew I wasn't a plant. Maybe this was real.

We all got out alive, obviously. Less obviously, we learned later that the brutality and sadism were structured to stop only when someone in the real audience cried out "Stop!" That night, the brave person who dared to stand and say enough was enough happened to be my brother-in-law's young date. It was a real-life lesson in fascism—that is, how much inhumanity will we permit as long as it's happening to someone else."[3]

Theatre of Cruelty indeed.

Gordon and Purdy continued to explore the boundaries of theatre by incorporating the language of film into their live productions. "Gordon's credo was, 'If it can be done on film, it can be done on stage, only better,'" wrote Christopher Sieving. Gordon and Kleinfeld produced *Warp!*, an audacious science-fiction parody that had three parts and grandiose sets. (*Warp!* was later adapted as a comic book series by First Comics.) For a production of *Hamlet*, Gordon tried to recreate the film experience through motion. "Instead of moving the sets, I moved the audience around on these bleachers that were on rollers...in for close-ups and back for long shots."[4]

"It's funny how things work out sometimes," Gordon told Gene Gregorits for the latter's book,

Midnight Mavericks. "*Re-Animator* was originally designed to be a production for the Organic Theater. I wanted to use our actors, and I wanted to shoot it in our theatre, using it as a soundstage. When the time came, when the production was ready to go, the board of the theatre got horrified by the idea."

Remember *E/R*? That play was a hit. It resulted in a broadcast TV series. The board members of the Organic fell in love with the success and exposure.

"[They] said, 'Organic should not be doing a horror movie. We should be doing an art film.' They did not want us to use the theatre to do [*Re-Animator*] or to attach Organic to it in any way. So, I ended up leaving. I took a leave of absence, came out here, and started shooting the movie in Hollywood. The members of the company felt like they had lost an

---

3   Winer, Linda. "Stuart Gordon, Chicago Theatre Thriller." *American Theatre*, 30 March 2020, https://www.americantheatre.org/2020/03/30/stuart-gordon-chicago-theatre-thriller/

4   Sieving, Christopher. "Stuart Gordon: Artist in Residence." *The University of Wisconsin-Madison*, https://archive.iarp.wisc.edu/stuart_gordon.html

opportunity. Then, Richard Fire, a member of the theatre company, wrote *Henry: Portrait of a Serial Killer* with John McNaughton. For John McNaughton. They used members of the company, including Tom Towles, Tracy Arnold [...] all great actors. They even used our production designer, Rick Paul, to do the film. So, *Henry* is more of Organic Theater more than *Re-Animator* is, although I was able to use my wife, Carolyn, in the film and one other member of the ensemble, Ian Patrick Williams. He plays a very brief role in the beginning, the Swiss doctor who discovers one of West's experiments in the pre-title sequence."[5]

---

5 Gregorits, Gene. *Midnight Mavericks*, P. 24 FAB Press 2007.

Stuart got the last laugh, of course, as he and Dean Schramm produced *Re-Animator: The Musical*, music and lyrics by Mark Nutter, in 2011.

Gordon was a man of many layers. Never forget that the man who exposed the hilarity lurking beneath the bloodiest horror also gave us the *Honey, I Shrunk the Kids* franchise.[6]

---

6 And while it's tempting to leave on the snarky "Theatre of Cruelty" remark here, I personally love that franchise, so, haters, like the fascists at the UW, can go screw.

Gordon does Hitchcock. (Photographer Unknown. All Rights Reserved)

TOM SULLIVAN SIDEBAR ON WARP!

"I lived in Wheaton, Illinois, as a teenager before I moved to Marshall, and one of my best friends was my art teacher, Mr. Lee. In 1972 or '73, during the summer, he called me and said, 'There's this play you've gotta see in Chicago. It's called *Warp!* It's a three-part comic book play.' The play starred John Heard. The programs were like little comic books. 'My body, my battlefield.' The theater was the Organic Theater, and it was a small building, like a storefront. They'd painted the interior black. For the seating, it looked like they'd stolen every baseball bench in a 10-mile radius. They didn't have a stage. There were two or three gym mats on the floor. It had 10-foot ceilings and was maybe 60 feet wide, maybe 30 feet deep. Not that big.

"They showed two parts per night. So, we saw parts One and Two one night, and then we came back the second night. They performed Part Three and then Part One again so they could get more shows per week. We're driving into Chicago for this. It was awesome! And it was filled with stunts and costumes. It was like 95 percent of it was up to your imagination because it was just black walls and gym mats. I sat in the front row, so people are hitting you as they go past, or props come bouncing at you.

"It's the story of a young advertising guy. He's getting married to the boss's daughter. He has a big presentation coming up. The pressure's on, and during the middle of his presentation, he starts flipping out. He has a nervous breakdown, because what is happening is 'Lord Cumulus' (his real identity) is coming

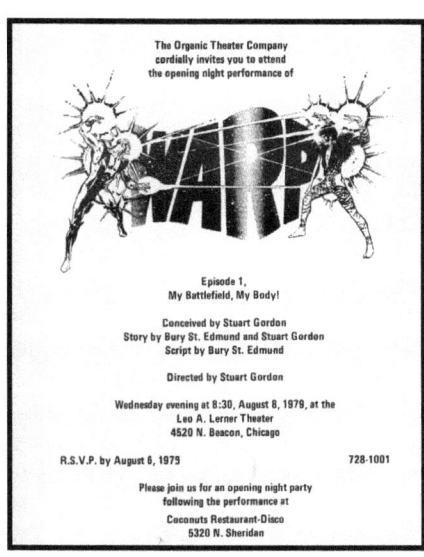

The Organic Theater Company cordially invites you to attend the opening night performance of

Episode 1,
My Battlefield, My Body!

Conceived by Stuart Gordon
Story by Bury St. Edmund and Stuart Gordon
Script by Bury St. Edmund

Directed by Stuart Gordon

Wednesday evening at 8:30, August 8, 1979, at the
Leo A. Lerner Theater
4520 N. Beacon, Chicago

R.S.V.P. by August 6, 1975   728-1001

Please join us for an opening night party
following the performance at
Coconuts Restaurant-Disco
5320 N. Sheridan

forward because God has died. The universe is going to fall into chaos because his nemesis, Prince Chaos, is coming for him. It turns out that not only must they battle, but they have to unite so that they can return sanity and order to the universe.

"So, Lord Cumulus is trained by Sargon, under the tutelage of Googlebondi, who was Obi-Wan before Obi-Wan. His legs were always folded on a platform, and they made it look like he was floating around the stage; the platform was draped with a curtain, with fake legs on the table, so he was really just walking around.

"Now, there's this net hanging over the stage that's held up by what looks like a giant lobster claw. It's up there the whole time. At one point, Prince Chaos and Lord Cumulus go to a planet and are threatened by an enormous, like, Godzilla-sized lobster man. And so, they have this 8-foot table—about 2 feet high. Our two heroes are standing on the table and go, 'Look out! The lobster man is reaching for us!' And they jump down behind the table and up pops two stick figure puppets, miniatures of the characters. So, they're doing the lines—the actors are puppeteering—and out steps this man in a ridiculous lobster costume. So, now he looks like a giant.

"He reaches for them, they blast him, and he topples off stage. Our actors pop back up and now we get to see why that net's been there the whole time. They release the claw and drop the net on the two actors. So, one rescues the other, and then they wrestle the claw offstage to be set up again for the next show. It was that kind of thing.

"At one point, they had to liberate this planet of slaves called the 'Pleebles.' They're working on these farms, producing these 'skleets,' blue bananas or something. The thing was, they grew the bananas, but they couldn't eat them. They had to buy them with their own money. So, they come in, get rid of the horrible corporation, and, of course, say the great chant from the '70s, 'The *skleets* belong to the *Pleebles*!'

"They took the play to New York, but they threw a lot of money at it, so it had all these dazzling spaceships and shit, and it just *bombed*. It worked so much better when it relied on your imagination.

"I did a Horrorhound out in Phoenix. It was the first time they did a show out there and [they] made a mistake. They booked the show in a hotel in the rich people's part of town. And then, later, they learned that the reason they did so badly was that the kids who would have attended—the kids without money—*hate* everyone from that part of town. It's a Phoenix thing. If they'd done it 3 miles down the road, they would have been mobbed. But instead, he lost his shirt. All these big stars—the cast of *Night of the Living Dead*, of *Day of the Dead*—what's the other one? *Dawn*. Tom Atkins was there. But because the attendance was so low, it was just three days of celebrities wandering around talking to each other. At one point, Stuart Gordon came over, and I just flipped. I did what I just did with you: I went through the entire play! I yelled, 'The *skleets* belong to the *Pleebles*!' and he goes, 'Oh, yeah, I forgot about that. That was a long way to go for a joke.'

"When *Evil Dead: The Musical* was going around, I'd seen it 22 times. I'd go backstage to hang out with the actors and the theatre folk, and I'd tell them about *Warp!* Every time, they'd ask, 'How do we get that?'

"It's really dated at this point, but I still think it would be fun to do. Somebody must have the rights to it. That could make a fun revival. It had this self-liberating spirit to it, connecting you to the cosmos."

NO RESPECT. NO RETURN. NO RESISTANCE: AN INTERVIEW WITH WRITER/DIRECTOR TIM THOMSON

by Ross Snyder

Houston, Texas, sometime in the near future. In the aftermath of a catastrophic collapse of America's governmental and financial infrastructures, Dij is a pink-haired, crank-snorting, Chinese-food-sauce-packet-devouring cyber-magician performing high-priced hacks-for-hire from his fully mobile, messenger-bag-style laptop. A disenfranchised veteran of the Russian-American war, Dij solely navigates a dystopian urban jungle, evading the ire of rival "government" street gangs and wielding his itinerant PC like a futuristic gunslinger. He erases phone bills and shuts down life-support systems for a bounty of drugs, floppy discs, or cold, hard cash (preferably Deutschmarks or something more stable than U.S. curren-

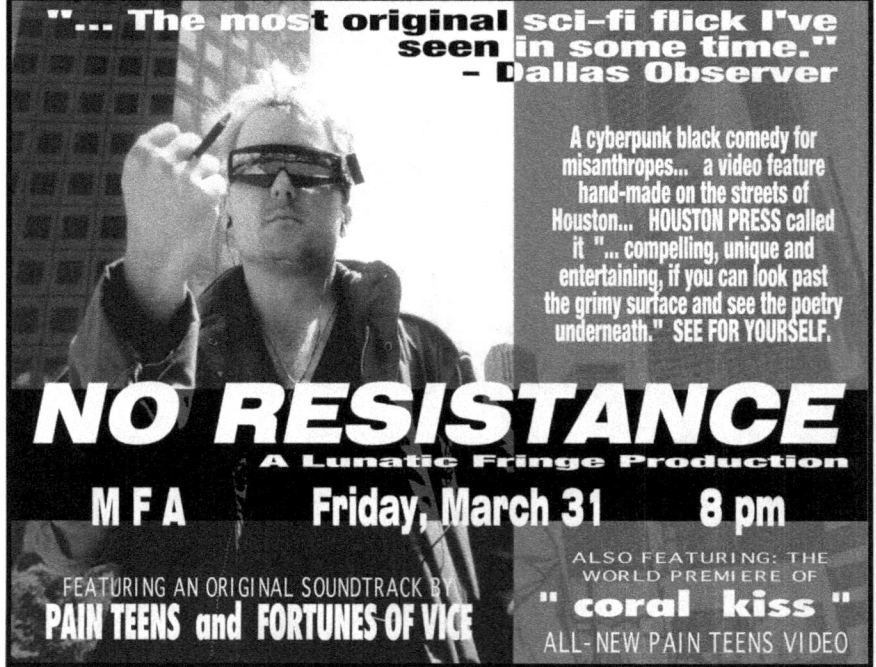

cy). When Dij is hired by a corporate crony to obtain a high-risk, weaponized computer virus, he finds himself inadvertently double-crossed and involuntarily implanted with a virus of a different kind: a lethal, infectious bioweapon, the fallout of which may lead to the end of all humanity as we know it.

While this may sound like the synopsis for an unreleased William Gibson manuscript, it's actually the plot of *No Resistance*, a highly inventive and virtually undiscovered shot-on-video masterpiece from 1994. Filmed guerrilla-style on SVHS for a paltry budget of just $7,000, *No Resistance* was the brainchild of Lunatic Fringe Productions, a Houston-based film collective composed of visionary director Tim Thomson and his imaginative writing and acting partners, David Rains and Irving Cutter. Released during the pinnacle of the second wave of the SOV feature phenomenon (an era defined by an intriguing new wave of innovative and accomplished video features like J.R. Bookwalter's *Ozone* and Scooter McCrae's *Shatter Dead*), *No Resistance* holds the distinction of being one of the few to use its lo-fi video aesthetic as an asset. Thomson's camcorder lens frequently transmogrifies into the watchful, encroaching eye of the technological "Big Brother," leering covertly through stoic computer monitors and security cams. A prophetic, futuristic knockout with a kinetic, industrial-noise rock soundtrack by Houston band Pain Teens, *No Resistance* stands apart in the shot-on-video echelon by dwelling unabashedly in the genre of science fiction. Like a dime-store *Blade Runner* by way of *Yojimbo* and filtered through the gritty lens of Ohio's Jim VanBebber, *No Resistance* remains one of the most iconoclastic cyberpunk, neo-noir sagas of the '90s, a saga created by a group of determined and innovative friends for a sum of money that would not have covered the catering costs on *Johnny Mnemonic*. I recently sought out director and cowriter Tim Thomson on behalf of *Exploitation Nation* for a retrospective discussion of the birth, death, and inevitable resurrection of *No Resistance*.

Ross Snyder: Growing up, what were some of the films that inspired you to pursue filmmaking?

Tim Thomson: I suppose that like many people in the DIY or indie film world, I was inspired by movies…lots and lots of movies. Although I originally always wanted to be a writer, there was a perfect storm of things in my younger years that always pointed me in the right direction. My parents both loved sci-fi and horror movies, and as a family, we never missed *Godzilla* on TV. There was a late-night horror movie host on WGN in the late '60s called Svengoolie, and I was always allowed to stay up and watch his show. Eventually, I started writing him and describing new movies he could make for us that were these terrible six-year-old's attempts at screenplays (complete with crayon illustrations). My dad owned a late-'60s Bolex Super 8mm camera that I used to create stop-motion experiments with army men and clay blobs in the sandbox. My dad allowed me to watch *Night of the Living Dead* when I was only four or five, and it really blew me away. Many from my generation always cite *Star Wars* as this huge touchstone influence, but for me, it was *Jaws*. I distinctly remember watching it and it suddenly dawning on me exactly what a director does—realizing that there was a way to tell a story that had a maximum effect on an audience, and choices about how to frame and pace things, and it was a job that someone could do. So, in the back of my mind, there was always the idea of making movies. I never dreamed that it could be achievable until I got out of high school, started working at a TV station, and found myself in the thrilling days of the VCR revolution.

RS: You moved to Houston after attending college. How did you get involved in the film/production scene there?

TT: In Corpus Christi, Texas, after high school, I worked my way through college at the local PBS station, which, during the time, was the smallest PBS station in the U.S. that was producing an enormous level of local programming (something like 10 to 12 hours of shows a week). I went from being a studio camera guy all the way up to head director, editor, and studio manager. We were so lucky then, like kids with the biggest train set ever. We didn't get paid much, but we all received an incredible three- to four-year education in real live TV. By 1989, I moved to Houston and have been here ever since. It was a logical shift to eventually go to the "big city" and try to get a real paying job. I couldn't get hired to a staff position, but I could do cheap grip work and get to know more and more folks in the industry. Due in part to the oil industry, there has always been a pretty large working community here. In 1991, I was hired on as an editor for a small video and film production company. Over the years, I worked my way up until I was a full partner (and the main writer/producer of the company), doing mostly industrial and corporate work. It was here where we had the base (employment with access to cameras, sound, and post) that would eventually make *No Resistance* possible.

RS: How and when did you hook up with *No Resistance* cowriter and star David Rains?

TT: I met David in high school in Corpus when I first got there in 1981. He and Irving Cutter (cowriter and producer of *No Resistance*) were a year ahead of me, but we hit it off immediately. David's mother, JJ Rains, was our theater and speech coach throughout high school, and she really became like a second mother to me (She eventually played the voodoo priestess in *Creaturealm: Demons Wake*). We all spent high school together, doing plays and debate tournaments, as well as hanging out at the local comic shop. We went to movies together and eventually started making our first rudimentary short films. Things really stepped up after high school when the TV station work came along. David worked at many stations then as well. By the time I moved to Houston, Irving Cutter was already there (having attended Rice University), and we each had two or three short films under our belt that were rough but definitely growing in complexity.

RS: *No Resistance* was originally conceptualized in 1989. What was the genesis of the project, and how did it eventually come to fruition under the Lunatic Fringe banner?

TT: After making a few shorts, we knew we wanted to tackle a feature, and we knew we wanted to make a real sci-fi film if we could. It gestated for a long time while we got used to living in Houston, but the inspiration grew out of a number of things at the time.

Shooting on Commerce Street. (All Photos this section courtesy and copyright Tim Thomson.)

We were all heavily influenced by the first wave of cyberpunk—literature like *Neuromancer* and *Mirrorshades* for sure, but also everything from underground punk zines to the *Semiotext€* journal, and even the music at the time. One of the biggest influences on the genesis of *No Resistance*, to be totally honest, was Sonic Youth's *Daydream Nation* album. So, we knew we wanted to make something in the vein of gritty, street-level, cyberpunk sci-fi. From there, it completely exploded from the brows of David Rains and Irving Cutter. I am credited with some screenplay work, but my contribution was mostly limited to cleanup and a few big picture notes. Irving Cutter studied history at Rice, and he built out an entire alternate U.S. history to base the story in (one that, in 1989-1990, was eerily prophetic). He predicted the 1991 Soviet coup d'état attempt to the month, as I recall. The screenplay really had a lot of great gestation time. It took about two years for Irv to craft this great world environment and for David to form the character of Dij. We molded the rest around a Dashiell Hammett plot and all the interesting locations we knew around town. In 1990, I bought a crappy, consumer-grade, $1,200 Magnavox SVHS camcorder and some really bad audio. In the summer of 1992, we put it all together and shot it over the course of three or four months for about $7,000 in hard costs. No one got paid. It was all materials, location rentals, costumes, and props. The taser was built to spec, and the computers were built out of old TI-99/4A's. We never really knew at the time how we would even complete post-production on it. We just got it on tape and hoped we'd figure it out later (about two years later, as it turned out).

RS: What would you say are some of the action or sci-fi films that inspired *No Resistance*?

TT: As I mentioned, the inspiration came mostly from print fiction. Maybe a little David Cronenberg. Maybe a little *Three Days of the Condor*. *Repo Man* and *Buckaroo Banzai* were big influences. At the time, I was obsessed with *Tetsuo: The Iron Man* and an '80s German industrial punk, sci-fi film called *Decoder* (which was made with folks from Einstürzende Neubauten and other notorious noise artists, prostitutes, and heroin junkies of the day). What really inspired a lot of the actual filmmaking decisions was more in the way of spaghetti westerns and early crime stuff. The entire plot outline was liberally lifted from Hammett's *Red Harvest*, which, of course, eventually became *Yojimbo* and *A Fistful of Dollars*. There's a long tradition in spaghetti westerns of antihero protagonists who live by a code but tend to err on the side of self-preservation and personal gain above all else.

RS: While the majority of SOV features of the era tend to present a certain rural charm, *No Resistance* is one of the few "metropolitan" features of the genre, with action taking place on the bustling streets, parking decks, and the high-rise offices of Houston. Since I'm guessing much of it was shot guerrilla-style, without permits, I'm sure you must have some interesting stories from the shoot.

TT: Oh yeah. All smash-and-grab and no asking for permission ever. The scene where Dij is cornered by the race militia in the parking structure was shot at my apartment complex around midnight. We ended up being noisy enough that someone called the police. A full HPD unit showed up and actually pulled weapons (We were heavily armed with fakes) and had us hit the ground. Once they saw it was all play, they actually got a real kick out of it. They offered to stay and hang out and even play parts if needed. That just can't happen anymore these days. The big multi-gang fight in the corporate office was all shot at a law firm we all worked at together in the early '90s. That was some of the last stuff we shot, and it just happened to be the night that the 1992 Republican National Convention was going on in Houston. The convention

The actual Magnavox that shot No Resistance.

was at the Astrodome far to the south, but we knew that a large convention office was in the building right next to us and was all shut down by security. It was hilarious that right across the way, we were staging this major gun battle.

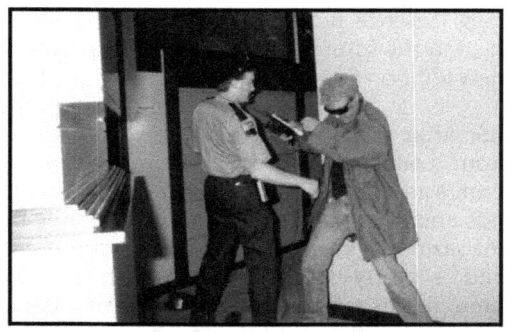

RS: Shot-on-video features seemed to have a predisposed negative stigma amongst certain audiences and critics at the time. However, I feel that *No Resistance* was one of the few that actually used the format to its advantage by incorporating many scenes visualized through computer monitors and security cameras. Was this envisioned as part of your aesthetic right from the get-go?

TT: Thank you so much. I really appreciate that because yes, that was our intention all along. It really started in the scripting phase. It was also heavily influenced by skateboard videos of the day. We saw those as maybe the only totally accessible thing that people watched all the time that didn't need slick production quality but still maintained a really fluid and dynamic, shot-from-the-hip style.

RS: *No Resistance* features a soundtrack by the Houston noise rock band Pain Teens. How did the soundtrack come about?

TT: Michael Schneider all the way. He was the music scene guy. He knew Bliss Blood (Pain Teens) from Sound Exchange, which was the premiere record store in those days. She, by extension, knew many other folks from bands in the scene, like Poor Dumb Bastards and Deadhorse, many of whom ended up playing roles in the movie. I had become a real fan of Pain Teens just by hearing them on college radio when I first moved here, so to have them interested in being a part of the movie just blew my mind. I can't thank them enough for taking the risk. They became really good friends, and we still work together to this day here and there. The music they made specifically for the film really changed the aesthetic of the film and had a huge overall impact.

RS: The floppy disks and Walkmans notwithstanding, your depiction of Dij's dark-web drug transactions and use of precursory AR smartglasses in *No Resistance* was astoundingly quite prophetic. What are your thoughts when reflecting on some of these surprisingly accurate technological predictions?

TT: Again, totally David and Irv. A lot of those things were already being explored in sci-fi at the time, but yeah, some of it is a bit eerie, right? It's pleasing to me that we found so many good hooks that didn't end up looking dumb in retrospect. Cellular access was another one. It's funny because it may have been a little too prophetic. Once the World Wide Web became a daily tool, much of the technologies connected to it became so ordinary and ubiquitous that they weren't even cool story points anymore. But like William Gibson himself said, "Science fiction isn't about predicting the future. It's about shining a new light on today."

RS: After a span of nearly five years from conceptualization to completion, aside from a few glowing write-ups and reviews in underground film magazines, it seems like *No Resistance* had a pretty scarce release at the time. Tell us a bit about the scope of the film's initial distribution and the overall difficulty of marketing a shot-on-video sci-fi feature in the mid-'90s VHS era.

TT: I wasn't really even aware of the DIY SOV scene when we started *No Resistance*. After the movie was done, we certainly learned a whole lot about it quickly. Distribution in the classic sense wasn't ever really a goal because we knew that the technical quality of the movie was kind of crap. We just thought we could sell copies ourselves in a limited boutique kind of way. Early zine reviews were good, but the showing at the Dallas Video Festival really changed everything. *No Resistance* was reviewed in the *Dallas Observer* by future Ebert film critic Matt Zoller Seitz, who also wrote a subsequent piece in the *Houston Press* and really put the movie on the local map. From there, local video and record stores started to carry it. The Museum of Fine Arts in Houston actually showed it as part of a local filmmakers series. Eventually, reviews from *Film Threat* and *Alternative Cinema* got the word out to the hip video stores in San Francisco, New York, and Los Angeles. We also took it personally to a lot of comic book conventions in the state. I also built a very early website, where I would highlight other cool video genre features. I met great folks like Kevin Lindenmuth, Mick McCleery, Michael Legge, Gabriel Campisi, Charles Pinion, Ron Ford, and other guys I thought were doing very fun stuff. Eventually, No Resistance was picked up by a small distributor out of Dallas called Scorpio. They were really behind it and enthusiastic, but I also don't think they were necessarily the right fit. They never really sold it, and from there, it sort of faded away. We just moved on to other stuff. We weren't kidding ourselves about it having a pretty short shelf life.

RS: You directed the "Possession Is Nine Tenths of the Law" segment in the 1998 SOV anthology *Creaturealm: Demons Wake*, equipped with another inventive script and performance from David Rains. I'm curious how you guys got involved with this project. Did you meet producer Kevin Lindenmuth after being profiled in his *Making Movies on Your Own* book?

TT: Kevin was kind enough to include the *No Resistance* story in his book based on an interview we did. He liked the special effects in the movie, which were very early, nascent works with After Effects. Those effects were just coming into their own but were something I was becoming really proficient with from corporate work. He was planning a lot of really ambitious stuff with his soon-to-be revealed *Alien Agenda* series, and I got invited to do a lot of early digital effects work on the first three. After those projects, Kevin asked us to submit a half-feature for his new *Creaturealm* series, and we jumped at the chance. As a joke, I mentioned I always wanted to make a courtroom drama because I found them so ridiculous and riveting. By now, our friend Michael Schneider was out of law school and a full-time, practicing lawyer, so it was natural for David to latch onto that and figure out a genre hook like he does so well. "Possession" was shot on Beta SP. We had graduated to pro formats by then, and it was a blast. The practical murder effects were so fucking arduous that I couldn't ask another real actor to go through the process, so I played the victim myself. All of it was shot in an actual courtroom by the way. Pretty sure I shouldn't say which one. I miss those days with Lindenmuth and his gang. I don't know why we dropped contact after all those years of working together. We had a great idea for a future *Alien Agenda* segment (from another kickass idea by Rains), but we ended up just not having the money or the time to effectively get it done right. Real life got weird. We gave up doing films and got way more into music and theatre.

RS: Several years after the feature, you produced a trailer for a potential *No Resistance* series. The future adventures of Dij amidst the fallout of the viral bioweapon potentially released at the denouement of the feature is certainly an enticing concept. How far along did you get with the series version?

TT: Scorpio, the distributor of *No Resistance*, was the genesis behind the idea of *No Resistance: The Series*. They were producing a low-budget documentary about science-fiction films and thought that if they had a pitch package for the series idea, they could get it in front of some possible cable folks, including the Syfy network. So, we worked up the trailer idea, and then David went to work plotting out a short season. He actually came up with a whole story arc and outlines for several episodes. They were to be an hour each and would always be titled something different but in a similar format: ("No Respect," "No Revelation," "No Reply," etc.). It just never got in front of anybody and probably would have looked ridiculous if it did. Good on them for trying, though. Out of that, David and I actually wrote a sequel feature script around 1997. Titled *No Return*, it was based on the pilot of the series, and it featured Dij in exile in Mexico after the events of the Houston pandemic. We had him fighting in the maquiladoras between armies of drug cartels and autonomous car manufacturers on the Texas-Mexico border, all while trying to get back into the States without alerting anyone. It was more of a futuristic spaghetti western, and it actually was a finalist in the Austin Heart of Gold screenplay festival. Unfortunately, it didn't win and never went further than the page. By 2015, I had been asked by people for a decade why we never produced a sequel to *No Resistance*. The answer was that the Internet age had made everything in it boring and obsolete. A historical Dij made no sense, until it did. David and I realized that if we could make it about that, it could totally work. Imagine Dij now in his alternate 2015, outmoded, outpaced, and totally made redundant by the Web, by Anonymous, by *World of Warcraft*, by iPad Pros. David once again wrote a kickass screenplay, called *No Reserve*. Imagine Logan but with Old Man Dij instead. Even then, we just weren't in the right spot to actually make it. It featured a lot of things about GPS hacking, autonomous drones, in-game economics, fooling image recognition systems, currency devaluation, the gig economy, etc. And now, in only five years, it itself is already totally obsolete. Go figure.

RS: I know you're still active in the industry today through your company, Hot Pixel Action. Tell us a bit about some of the projects you've been working on recently. Has there been

93

any desire to return to the director's chair for another micro-budget feature over the years?

TT: I've been lucky in that I still get paid to make films, but, of course, mostly of the corporate variety. By the very end of the 1990s, we got very burned out. It seemed like people were making movies all the time in Houston, but none of them was very good, and they all had huge expenses and very little return. As I said, we started getting way more interested in doing music and theatre. I had an experimental electronic project with Mike Schneider for a while called dr:op:fr:am+e. The company I worked for went under, and I went freelance for a while, went through a divorce, and rebuilt everything again into Hot Pixel Action, which I ran with my now wife. That eventually became part of a larger agency called Staging Solutions, and we put all our energy into that.

The interesting news over the last year is that we finally obtained an option for the rights to a novel I have always wanted to make a feature of (from way back to the 1988-1989 era). It's a 1951 weird sci-fi/mystery/thriller novel, and we purchased the option last fall. We're working on the screenplay right now. I don't know what will become of it. Back in the '90s, everything felt possible. Now it seems nearly impossible to make anything with a decent-sized budget and still find a market for it. I don't really want to make it on a micro budget. I'd love to figure out a way to get a few million and shoot it on film, but is that even possible anymore? Who knows? But I'm excited about the script possibilities, and maybe, just maybe, we'll be back in production in the next year or so. Fingers crossed.

RS: With the pending VHS rerelease of *No Resistance* (courtesy of Saturn's Core Audio & Video) and the inevitable rediscovery of the film by a new generation of fans, what are your overall thoughts on *No Resistance* looking back at it nearly 25 years after its release?

TT: I am so gratified that people still find *No Resistance* interesting. I don't know how that could be the case exactly, but I am. I think it speaks to the power of the story and characters in the film that people can ignore how technically terrible it is. Like the man says, it's all about the script, and at the very least, it is very much of its time. I'm very proud that we, all of us, were able to make something out of nothing.

The VHS release of No Resistance can be found here: https://saturn-scoreaudiovideo.bigcartel.com/

BIZARRO FILM DEPARTMENT: TAMMY, TANNY, SOMEONE'S IN LOVE

Indie distribution may have collapsed upon itself, but outfits like Vinegar Syndrome and Severin Films have been mining the cinematic dregs of the past and uncovering some true gems, as well as some truly baffling offerings. *Tammy and the T-Rex* (1994) is the latter. Like the insane John Stamos/Gene Simmons spy movie *Never Too Young to Die*, *Tammy* is a movie that has to be experienced.

Here's the rundown: Tammy (Denise Richards, in her first film) is dating Michael (*The Fast and the Furious*' Paul Walker, in his third film). Her former boyfriend, Billy (George Pilgrim in *his* first film), doesn't like this. During the fight, the two of them grab each other's balls, and neither feels any desire to let go. Billy also dislikes Tammy's gay best friend, Byron (Theo Forsett, in his last movie).

Denise Richards and co-star discuss their craft.
(All photos this section Copyright Greenline Productions. All Rights Reserved.)

Meanwhile, Dr. Wachenstein (Terry Kiser, in his 20th movie) has an animatronic T-Rex. For some reason, he wants to put a human brain in it. Because sentient robot dinosaurs are the future liberals want. Or something. His assistant, Helga (Ellen Dubin, in her third film), doesn't get it either. But, fortunately, Billy and his gang (which also includes Sean Whalen as "Weasel," whose other roles include "Roach," "Wormser," and "Merkin") chase Michael down and throw him into a lion pen at the zoo (!). Wachenstein declares Mauled Michael legally dead so that he can harvest the young dope's brain for his Dinobot. Hilarity ensues when Michael escapes to track down both his Tammy and his attempted, albeit creative, murderers. It gets funnier when Tammy realizes that it's Michael with the tiny arms and massive teeth, and she vows to help him find a better body to inhabit.

This movie is the product of the mind of Stewart Raffill. Name doesn't ring a bell? How about one of his other projects: *Mac and Me*? *The Ice Pirates*? Raffill's bizarrely composed mind created both of those puzzling entertainments. So, it would be incorrect and disingenuous to call Raffill a "bad" director. Whatever you think of those low-budget-hampered movies, they are more bizarre than anything else. (I find *Mac and Me* unwatchable in the same way as autopsy footage, and I can't really describe the aversion; it's more uncomfortable than misguided.) Raffill grew up in post-blitz England. At the age of 19, he immigrated to the U.S. with the intention of getting into movies. He wound up as an animal trainer first, which explains the lion sequence in *Tammy*. Through the animal training grapevine, Raffill met Fernando Celis, another trainer and stunt man, which eventually led to *Tammy*, which I consider destiny.

Celis had a buddy who owned theaters in South Africa, and this guy was sending a new attraction to a theme park in Texas: an animatronic dinosaur.

…Oh, you wanted more? What additional incentive would any indie filmmaker need? Fine. The owner was about to sell the silly thing, and a three-week window opened for Raffill and Celis to use the dinosaur in a movie. So, in true indie fashion, a movie was written around it. Celis found the producers, but he had a caveat that the movie had be made for under a million dollars, which seems like a reasonable request considering the script (cowritten by Gary Brockette) was the vehicle for a prop. Raffill had a requirement of his own: To further keep costs down, the film had to be shot within a 20-mile radius of his home in Thousand Oaks, Calif. Raffill's wife, Diane, would produce.

Now, nothing I've written so far does justice to the true weirdness of this movie. The upbeat and absurd *Saved by the Bell* tone, combined with ridiculous gore, puts it in a weird category to start. (The plot alone sounds like a Steve Urkel scheme.) The effects range from amazing to "I had 10 minutes, fuck-face!" The fake Michael body used during the brain-removal sequence is pretty terrific. When Dino picks gore out of its teeth, we realize that sometimes its arms are much longer than you'd normally find on your average household tyrannosaurus.

Kiser, of course, leaves no scenery unchewed, so he is a great asset to the absurdity. As Billy, Pilgrim is less villainous and more in need of balanced medication. ("I didn't want to be in a movie where I got my head bitten off; I was really superstitious at the time!" he said on the DVD, out loud and everything.)

But then you get Walker and Richards, who are playing their upbeat, unflappable teens with the utmost absurdity. Walker is sincere for the entire run of his pre-eaten existence. Richards has literally never been better. She totally delivers the pitch-perfect cheerleader-in-love-with-a-robot-dinosaur-with-her-boyfriend's-brain-in-it. There is nothing silly about this teen romance. The scene where the dinosaur explains to Tammy, via charades, that it has Michael's brain is jaw-dropping. Her emoting to the dying animatronic dinosaur must be seen. Her dénouement lingerie dance to a brain in a fish tank is a master class in surrealism. At one point in the film, Tammy crosses herself before "going into battle." (As Richards states in the Blu-ray doc, "With every film I do, I always expect to get fired," which is a pretty apt summary of Denise Richards.)

Raffill had a ride-or-die philosophy during production. As the film was shot in '93 during the Calabasas fires, smoke and flames are visible in the

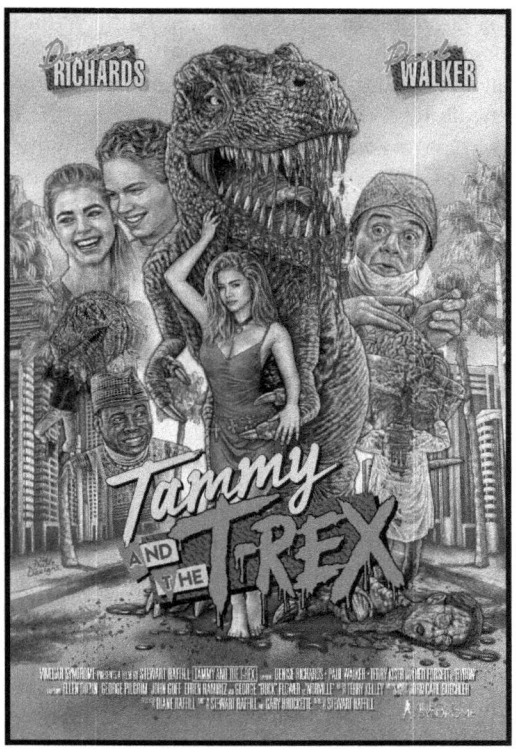

background during the sequence where Tammy escapes astride Dino-Mike. When the production was told to evacuate, Director of Photography Cliff Toleman bribed the fire marshal for more time. The fire marshal shrugged his shoulders and took the money.

Now, if I haven't sufficiently enticed you with the film, allow me to turn your attention to the extras on the Vinegar Syndrome Blu-ray. It is a rare and precious miracle when the interviews are weirder than the movie. Raffill, for instance, comes off initially as a sincere, earnest man describing his art. But every story he tells takes a weird left-turn down a digression lane. While discussing the fires and boasting how he kept his crew in immediate danger, Raffill begins to first complain about how lawyers and the insurance companies "swallowed" Hollywood, and then to warn everyone listening about the evils of global warming. He relates the gore in the film to his time working on a farm in the Midwest as a teenager. The slaughterhouse stories he recalls are more graphic than the film. Did you know that editor Terry Kelly was Raffill's housemate and started as a tree-trimmer? They worked for another neighbor, who….

The finished *Tammy* was reedited for U.S. distribution, removing much of the gore to obtain a PG-13 rating. The Euro cut retained that gore, and that's the version Vinegar Syndrome delivers. But there's even another layer. Celis lived in South America and reedited "certain aspects of the film to make it make sense" for South American audiences. Raffill chalks this up to Celis being "in his '70s" and not understanding the sci-fi aspects.

This is the official explanation for why the on-screen title is *Tanny and the Teenaged T-Rex*. It does not explain why certain characters actually call Tammy "Tanny."

Raffill then blames Universal for doing the same thing to *The Ice Pirates*, claiming that the studio head went into the editing room and reedited it the day before they ran the prints, removing the ending where the pirates reach modern-day Malibu. Raffill feels this hurt his legacy. "You're immortalized by your films, and these are not your films."

Which is a fair point. Immortality is a weird sub-theme of *Tammy* as well. May we all be lucky enough to live on in the bodies of animatronic dinosaurs.

WHAT OUR FRIENDS ARE UP TO

We know a lot of interesting, talented people. Here are some of them.

Unless noted, these can be had for a modest price through Amazon, who tells us that it loves us and want us to be happy, and who are we to argue?

Medium Chill: The brainchild of *EN*'s Dr. Rhonda Baughman, *Medium Chill* quietly harkens back to the freeform style of literary and poetry zines, with its many authors exploring no end of themes. Poems, thought experiments, short stories, cartoons—there's a little something for everyone in there.

Tall and Short Tales of My Hometown, by Carmine Capobianco: *Psychos in Love* star Capobianco was never shy about his love for Waterbury, Conn. This love letter to small-town life is charming and wonderful and should be incorporated as PR by the Waterbury Chamber of Commerce. With chapters like

"The Bombshell of Waterbury" and "The Mad Bomber Killed Nobody," this book falls comfortably between Lake Wobegon and S.J. Perelman (with more than a little Jean Shepherd).

Crazy (2020), written and directed by Holt Boggs. An "ill-equipped" man meets with an eccentric hit man to take out his wife's lover. Presumably over penis issues. Then things get stranger.

Essentially a two-man conversation between Boggs (so marvelous in Will Kaufman's *The Prodigy*) and Brian Villalobos (*Bit Parts*), *Crazy* goes down smooth with some hilarious dialogue and wonderfully-eccentric performances by the two leads. Check out more at www.holtboggs.com

Wives of the Skies (2020), written and directed by Honey Lauren (*Satan was a Lady*), this short film set in 1965 involves Fran and Marcy (Rachel Alig, Maddison Bullock, both terrific), stewardesses for the airline Fine Air, and a budding friendship they strike up with an oily British photojournalist (Drew Brandon Jones) who wants them as interview subjects in his "documentary film." But when he joins them in their hotel room, he discovers a relationship between the two women he was not prepared for. From the official PR: "As they get to know each other, *Wives of the Skies* makes a contemporary socio-cultural statement regarding the meme of "the good girl, drawn bad". *Wives of the Skies Clarifies* the impact of the overarching "men's gaze" which objectifies women as carnal sex objects men seek, while they look for love... along the way, addressing the primitive issue of Trust vs. Mistrust, Wives of The Skies displays the Japanese art of Kinbaku."

According to Lauren in her Director's statement: "When someone I know sent me a link to vintage 1960's Stewardess outfits for sale on EBay, I was blown away at not only the popularity and high prices, but that these outfits are sold, collected and bid on, by what looked like mostly men. I recognized that these uniforms have become a fetish...for me, at the very least unexpected. Curious, I researched the history of stewardesses during this particular era. The stewardesses were sporting uniforms by top fashion designers like Pucci, Mary Wells and Yves Saint Laurent. The fabrics, which "hugged" as they stretched, were considered revolutionary for their ability to display the stewardesses [...] something about these "sexy Stewardesses", seemed pushed and insincere. [...] I have long recognized that where there is a pattern, there is a story. *Wives of the Skies*, is a story. And a question... 'Sex sells, but at what cost?'

With the period lovingly recreated (kudos to costumer, Stephanie Scull), beautifully shot by Davey Robertson, *Wives of the Skies* is a beautiful and surprising short.

Check out more at wivesoftheskies.com

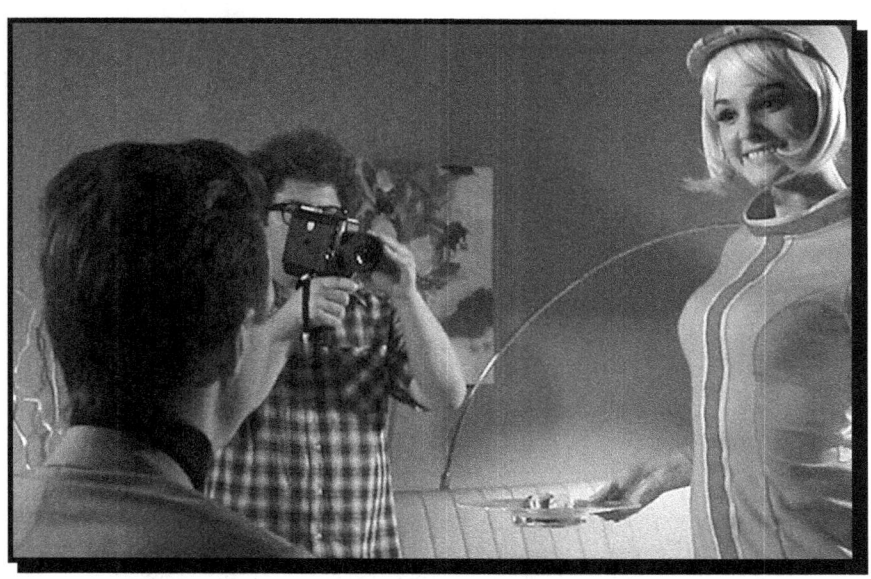

L-R Drew Brandon Jones, Sebastian Fernandez, and Maddison Bullock in Honey Lauren's Wives of the Skies.

MORE FRIENDS WITH BOOKS! ON SALE NOW!

From Jim Towns

From Pete Chiarella and HCM, LLC

"This is a cool idea for a book." — Quentin Tarantino

My Best Friend's Birthday: The Making of a Quentin Tarantino Film is the story of a group of friends who set out to make their own movie in 1983, financing it with Tarantino's minimum wage earnings from his job at a video store. In most biographies and Tarantino histories, this unfinished $5,000 film is mentioned only in passing and is looked upon as little more than a curiosity. But with this oral history, author/editor Andrew J. Rausch details how each of the friends came together, other early film projects they worked on, and how they ended up making (or trying to make) a black-and-white screwball comedy.

He also makes the argument that *My Best Friend's Birthday* is something far more meaningful than a curiosity. Not only did it mark the screenwriting and directorial debut of Quentin Tarantino, one of the greatest filmmakers in history, but it also launched the careers of two other professional filmmakers, Craig Hamann and Roger Avary. **My Best Friend's Birthday: The Making of a Quentin Tarantino Film** provides an in-depth look at the film from its conception to its eventual demise and proves that even at the young age of 20, Tarantino already possessed the talent (in a still rough, unpolished form) that would lead him to make classic films such as *Reservoir Dogs, Pulp Fiction, Kill Bill, Django Unchained,* and *Once Upon a Time in...Hollywood*. The film and screenplay for *My Best Friend's Birthday*, rough as they may be, provide us a glimpse of an artist on the verge of real success, still trying to find and hone his voice.

Available in paperback, hardback, and Kindle at *Amazon.com*
or order directly from *bearmanormedia.com*.

From Andy Rausch

I'D BUY THAT FOR A DOLLAR!
by Mike Haushalter

One of my favorite activities is to look through bargain bins and the racks of second-hand sellers to find movie deals. Whether it's a forgotten A-list title, blink and you missed indie release, or last year's hot direct to home video title, as long as it costs 2 to 5 bucks it's bound to come home with me. But if it's less than that? Well, I'm willing to take a gamble on almost anything that's priced at a dollar and offers even a tiny bit of intrigue or interest. After all, I can't even rent most of these things for that price, and if they don't work out, I can bin them up and trade them in. But when they do work out, it's magical.

At some point in mid 2019 I started to see Facebook posts about fellow fans making amazing Blu-Ray finds at dollar stores. As this information was very relative to my interests and my column in this fine magazine I began haunting my local dingy dollar stores to see what I could find. My first few of these quests were fruitless, other than stumbling across a copy of Hobo With A Shotgun, which I didn't want to view a second time even for a dollar. But when the Christmas season rolled in I started to find a few winners (or losers depending on how you look at it) and I scored some good titles for review. I also got two ¥100 Yen (pretty much the Japanese version of a dollar) films to review, courtesy of my wife which she picked up while at a showing of her art in Japan.

Here's a roundup of my latest discoveries and my souvenirs from Japan:

. . . .

All Cheerleaders Die (2014)
The box says: Teenage outsider Maddy (Caitlin Stasey, *I, Frankenstein*) is keeping some dark secrets and holding a serious grudge against the captain of the Blackfoot High football team. When Maddy joins the school's elite and powerful cheerleading squad, she convinces her new friends to help inflict her revenge. After a late-night party goes awry, their plans take an unexpected

turn for the worst and all of the girls die. A sinister, supernatural power intervenes and the girls mysteriously appear at school the next day with a killer new look... and some unusual new appetites. "Sexy, campy, funny, subversive, angsty and most importantly fun" (*The Hollywood Reporter*) ALL CHEERLEADERS DIE is a rebellious horror-comedy that redefines the genre. Written and directed by Lucky McKee and Chris Sivertson.

Why I risked a dollar: I kind of bought this one out of desperation after not finding anything of merit after half a dozen or so trips to the dollar store. I mean the box makes it look kind of cool and I may have heard of it before I found it but now that it comes time to write about it I can't think of a legitimate reason for it coming home with me.

Thoughts: *All Cheerleaders Die* is a very busy teen horror film that seems to take forever to get started.and once it does get started it quickly falls apart. I am not sure if it's just that I am not the film's intended audience or what but I found it very hard to get through and I find it hard to believe this was intended for theatrical release. With that in mind it is hard to see who this aimed at it is hyper sexual and violent yet the horror elements are straight out of a *Goosebumps* book.

Plus: Some good strutting and poseing. Fairly decent portrayal of Lesbianism.

Minus: Kind of a silly premise. Charmless cast and unlikable characters. Subpar special effects. laughingly bad CGI blood Unfavorable/ignorant portrayal of Wiccans. Lack of adults or police noticing anything at all.

Shelf/Bin: It's in the bin and out the door.

* * * * * * * * * * * *

Kickboxer: Vengeance (2016)
The box says: Jean-Claude Van Damme returns for a new chapter in the adrenaline-charged *Kickboxer* legacy. Kurt Sloane (Alain Moussi) has always been there for his brother, Eric (Darren Shahlavi), who's known in the martial arts world as a modern-day warrior. But when the ruthless and undefeated fighter Tong Po (David Bautista) brutally ends Eric's life in a no-holds-barred match in Thailand,

Kurt devotes himself to training with a master (Van Damme) in a quest for redemption... and revenge. Featuring MMA champions Georges St-Pierre, Gina Carano, Cain Velasquez and Fabricio Werdum, *Kickboxer: Vengeance* delivers a one-two punch of jaw dropping fights and death-defying stunts.

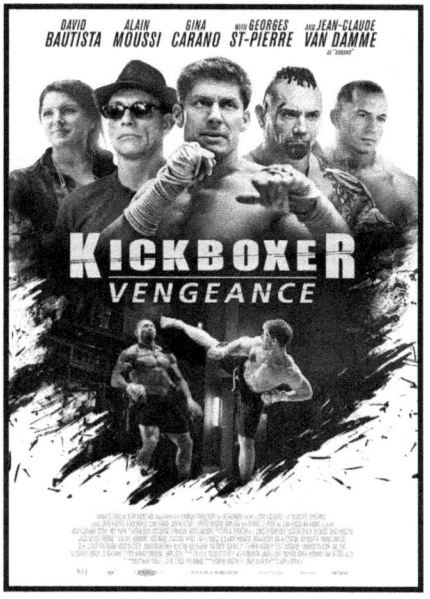

Why I risked a dollar: Figured a dollar for a brand new Blu-ray starring Bautista would be made of win. The rest of the cast list sounded pretty promising as well.

Thoughts: Mostly joyless bloodsport-style martial arts outing. I guess I should have expected as much from a remake of *Kickboxer* which, beyond Van Damme, didn't have much going for it. I think I would have enjoyed this much more if someone other than Alain Moussi would have had the lead role. Alain Moussi is a top notch on screen fighter to be sure perhaps even better than Van Damne but he has none of Van Damme's on screen presence or charisma and is as bland as stewed cabbage.

Plus: Plenty of martial arts punch ups. Jean-Claude Van Damme is in top shape, shows off some decent fight moves and is surprisingly funny. David Bautista is a fantastic villain. Funny end credits stinger. Fantastic Easter eEgg joke for fans of the original *Kickboxer*.

Minus: Charisma free leading man. Gina Carano has no fight scenes. Bautista should have had more screen time. Despite the number of good fights the film never seems very fun or exciting and unless Van Damme or Bautista is on the screen it is pretty dull going..

Shelf/Bin: As much as I like Bautista and Van Damme, I really don't think I will want to revisit it any time soon or even later so into the box it goes.

Lady Bloodfight (2016)

The box says: When Jane, a beautiful but troubled American backpacking her way through Hong Kong, successfully fends off three thugs trying to rob her, it draws the attention of Shu, a female fighting champion. Shu recruits and trains Jane to fight in the vicious, all-female underground martial arts tournament known as The Kumite. After months of rigorous training, Jane is ready to face off against her killer rivals, including the apprentice of Shu's nemesis, a Shaolin master. As other nefarious forces emerge from the shadows, Jane's journey through The Kumite turns deadly as she risks everything to become the best female fighter in the world.

Why I risked a dollar: I picked this one up the same day I picked up *Kickboxer: Vengeance*. I like female fight flicks and I thought the two films would make a decent kumite double feature. Another plus (at least I thought it was when I picked it up) was that kung fu movie scribe Bey Logan was part of the production.

Thoughts: Female blood sport outing in the vein of *Angel Fist* or *Kickboxer* that's full of decent fighters but short on warmth and charm. Not much to report here other than that in my research it looks like Bey Logan's dream cast fell through. Also there were some money problems so maybe a better movie could have been made, but I doubt it and it sounds like Logan is to blame.

Plus: Wall-to-wall martial arts mayhem. Strong female cast who all look tough, sexy, and competent. Never feels like an exploitation film.

Minus: Mean-spirited and insipid. Super unbelievable comebacks: I mean I know the heroes got to win and all, but Christ, at one point the heroine took a beating that would have put Hulk Hogan down for the count yet still comes out on top.

Shelf/Bin: Yeah this really is not a keeper, it's not very fun and the fights while plentiful are just humdrum.

• • • • • • • • • • • • •

U.M.A. 2010
on screen title: Rise of the Gargoyles (2009 TV Movie)

The box says: A monster panic movie depicting the horror of a mysterious unidentified creature who suddenly comes flying and chops its prey by making it unidentified. Jack, an American scholar teaching at a university in Paris, witnesses an unidentified monster while exploring a cathedral graveyard of a church near the demolition. After

that night, mysterious murders continued in the city of Paris. It was the work of unidentified creatures sealed in the catacombs.

Why my wife risked a ¥100yen: "I was in Japan for a week-long conference, in a small town where most of the shops near the conference center and the hotel were only open during conference hours. Lucky for me one of the few places open late was a music store with tables of miscellaneous stuff in the middle, where I found a small cache of used DVDs. I didn't have any translation software on my phone, and while I speak Japanese enough to manage short transactions, I can't read it well. After several international texts I went on the last day of my stay to pick out a couple of movies for Mike. I was attracted to this one by the crazy cover, which has something that's definitely not the Bat Signal passing through a skyscraper, and it didn't look like a *Ringu* knockoff."

Thoughts: My wife traveled halfway around the world and one of the treasures she found was a DVD copy of a Syfy channel movie of the week? Well you certainly wouldn't have guessed that from the box art that makes it look like some sort of awesome Kaiju movie that was never released here in the states. On the plus side it's not a bad movie in fact it's a pretty decent time waster.

Plus: Amazing box art. Fun opening trailer reel (the one for *Man of the East - Mission: Ultimate,* a Russian *Transporter* knock-off, was my favorite). Great on screen beheading, pretty good story line, a fine cast including Eric Balfour (*Skyline*), Tanya Clarke (*Banshee*) and Nick Mancuso (*Rapid Fire*).

Minus: It's a Syfy channel movie of the week. Poor Monster effects. Been there done that storytelling

Shelf/Bin: This one's a keeper not only for its cool box and sentimental value, but also because it's a pretty fun rainy day monster movie kind of flick.

* * *

Septic Man (2013)
The box says: Water pollution of unknown origin occurred in a rural Canadian town. The damage spreads quickly, and the inhabitants are vomited and diarrhea attacked one after another. Asked to find out what

107

caused the pollution, the plumber, Jack, overcame the opposition of his pregnant wife and went on to investigate the sewer. Unfortunately, Jack accidentally stinks

Why my wife risked a ¥100yen: I was attracted to this one for the cover that gave me a Frankenstein's monster vibe. And again, it wasn't a Ringu rip-off, as most of the DVDs in the shop that weren't J-pop or K-pop concerts looked to be.

Thoughts: Low-budget super bleak bio-terror film that was made perhaps a bit bleaker for me because I watched it during the quarantine. This is a perfect film to name drop when that guy on your horror group asks for the most grueling film possible. It's not *A Serbian Film,* mind you, but it's a messy, foul, retched outing that may prompt you to head to the showers.

Plus: It's gruelingly horrific. Great low light photography, everything is dark but you can still see all the important things. Locations and or sets look very real and so filthy. Really good looking film. Gruesome makeup effects and gore. End credits song.

Minus: Why does the hero go into a sewer to seek out a source of water contamination without any protective gear of any sort. Long grueling scenes of man stuck in garbage filled sewer water muck. So much vomit.

Shelf/Bin: I will be keeping this for at least a bit. It's a great film to showcase the next time I get together with friends for man's inhumanity to man movie night and a fun memento from my wife's trip to Japan.

Back issue pages like REAL magazines used to have!
I mean, ALSO FROM HAPPY CLOUD MEDIA, LLC:

Exploitation Nation—Premiere Issue! We kick off with everyone's favorite sub-genre: the **Lesbian Vampire Film**. In this premiere issue, Dyanne Thorne interview; "lost" interviews with Clive Barker and his *Saint Sinner* stars, Mary Mara, Rebecca Harrell. Plus reviews! $5.99

#2: Cryptids of the Cinema: Bigfoot, Nessie, The Mothman, The Yeti, The Pope Lick Monster - we got 'em all! Well, most. The monsters and the movies that love them. Also this issue, journalist Mike Watt takes a look back at his time covering 2009's *Sorority Row*. Plus, bidding a fond farewell to **George A. Romero**. $7.99

#3: Bizarro Films. Contributions from Heather Drain and John Skipp. PLUS: Jose Mojica Marins, aka "Coffin Joe"; an interviews with filmmakers Rolfe Kanefsky; Greg DeLiso and Peter Litvin, and EXCLUSIVE INTERVIEW with Stephen Sayadian (aka "Rinse Dream"). $7.99

#4: Rock 'n Roll Movies! 144-pages! Interviews with Paul Bunnell (*The Ghastly Love of Johnny X*); Jon-Mikl Thor and Frank Dietz (*Rock 'n Roll Nightmare*); *Slade in Flame*; AIP's *Beach Party* films; Prince on Film; goodbye to Harlan Ellison; Richard Elfman on *Forbidden Zone*. $7.99

#5: Alternate Reality Warning: not a single title in this book is real. Interviewee Larry Blamire ("The Lost Skeleton Cadavra") is real, but the interview isn't. Plus: The Beatles' adapt *Lord Of The Rings*, directed by Stanley Kubrick; David Lynch directs *Revenge of the Jedi*; Amos Poe's remake of *Alphaville* with Debbie Harry; the film adaptation *A Field Guide To Film Gods*. ALL HAIL CINEMAGOG! $7.99

#6: Underground Comix! Did your old man throw YOURS away? Interviews with: Stephen Bissette, Trina Robbins, Mike Diana, Frank Henenlotter, Greg Ketter, Mark Bode, Howard Cruse's final interview; plus Buddy Giovinazzo, Vaughn Bode's final essay, *Confessions Of A Cartoon Gooroo*; Spaghetti Westerns, Robert Altman's *Popeye*, and a eulogy for Stan Lee.

Note: #6 Boasts two covers, sold separately:

COVER A - Mark Bode's mural from San Francisco's Clarion Alley.

COVER B - Will Eisner's art for Denis Kitchen's SNARF #3. $7.99 each

#7: Indie Filmmaking issue! * Mark Savage and his new film *Purgatory Road*; James L. Edwards and *Her Name Was Christa*￼ Gabe Bartalos and his newest, *Saint Bernard*￼ Scooter McCrae and his adventures with the British censorship; Carmine Capobianco (*Psychos in Love*); Henrique Couto (*Babysitter Massacre*); Revjen Miller (*The Adventures of Electra Elf*). $7.99

#8: Witnesses for the Defense! Our writers to defend a movie only they seem to like. From *Grease 2* to *Ernest Goes to Jail* to *Godzilla '98*. PLUS an **exclusive interview with director Terry Gilliam** and *The Man Who Killed Don Quixote*! $7.99

Grindhouse Purgatory #12 is a special ALL SOMETHING WEIRD VIDEO Issue paying tribute to that all-important label we know and cherish. Contents include memories of SWV founder Mike Vraney; tributes to Herschell Gordon Lewis, David F. Friedman; a word from Frank Henenlotter; a look at those Sexy Shockers, Drivers-Ed, and Health Scare films, and much, much more! $9.99

GP #15: In this special issue, we say goodbye to our friend, actor, and mentor, Sid Haig. His friends and fans come from all over contribute remembrances of this amazing man and his incredible career. From his early days starring in Jack Hill's exploitation epics, to his resurgence in *Jackie Brown* and *House of 1,000 Corpses*, Sid was a unique performer and a lovely person. $9.99

Grindhouse Purgatory Greatest Hits: collecting the best material from the now out-of-print Issues 1-3, along with some brand new material unavailable anywhere else. Spaghetti Westerns! Hardcore Wrestling! *Codename: Wild Geese*! The forgotten beauty of '70s 42nd Street! Plus a little tribute to our departed friend, Andy Copp. And much more! $9.99

Night of the Living Dead '90: The Version You've Never Seen by Tom Savini. Take a look at the intended version of Tom Savini's remake of *Night of the Living Dead 1990*, thorugh this unique book collecting the full storyboards for this film for the first time. Thirty years after the fact, the true story can be told. With annotations by the director and exclusive photographs! This is a unique look at a classic film. $29.99

Shadows & Light: Journeys With Outlaws in Revolutionary Hollywood by Gary Kent. Writer, director, actor, stuntman, special effects guru, production manager Gary Kent tells his Hollywood story, chronicling his adventures with Brian De Palma, Bruce Campbell, Ed Wood, Charles Manson, Frank Zappa, the Hells Angels and others. This is the first printing from Happy Cloud Media, LLC, with an updated Afterword. $19.99

A Whole Bag of Crazy: Sordid Tales of Hookers, Weed, and Grindhouse Movies by Pete Chiarella. Hustler, pot fiend, porn expert.Take a walk down a dark alley with 42nd Street Pete as he recounts his tales growing up on "The Deuce". Criminal activity, classic undesirable cinema, pot, booze, pros, cons. The '70s: uncut, uncensored. If you really remember the '70s, you were lucky to have survived them. $14.99

Movie Outlaw: The Prequel by Mike Watt is a revamped republishing of what was previously-known as *Fervid Filmmaking*. Featuring essays on 70 underseen films including *Keep Off My Grass, Dr. Caligari, Forbidden Zone, Coonskin, Head, Psychos in Love*, and many more. A rare interview with director Stephen Sayadian. 350 pages. $15.99

Movie Outlaw by Mike Watt. Essays focusing on more than 70 underseen films including Johnny Depp's directorial debut, *The Brave*; *Don's Plum*; Mauritzio Nichetti's *Volere Volare*; *The Ghastly Love of Johnny X*, the last 35mm black 'n white science fictional musical ever made! 472 pages. $19.99

Movie Outlaw Rides Again! By Mike Watt. Essays on 70 underseen films: *Crazy Moon*; *Frankenhooker*; *Jane White is Sick and Twisted*; *The Magic Christian*, *Meet the Feebles*; *Impure Thoughts*; *The Stunt Man*; *Night Breed*; Brian DePalma's *Phantom of the Paradise*, Will Vinton's *The Adventures of Mark Twain*; *The Redsin Tower*. 392 pages. $19.99

Son of the Return of Movie Outlaw by Mike Watt. Essays include: *Accion Mutante;* Ralph Bakshi's *Heavy Traffic*; *Down and Dirty Duck*; *The Thief and the Cobbler*; *The Sinful Dwarf*; *Performance*; *Muppets Most Wanted*; *Legend of Simon Conjurer*; *Sorority Babes in the Slimeball Bowl-O-Rama*; *Shock Treatment*; *Yellowbeard*. Interviews with Jon Voight and Ralph Bakshi! 352 pages. $19.99

Hot Splices by Mike Watt. Eight interwoven tales about the Film Addicts, the Cinephages who devour film for the high, the bleeding perforations in their skin is just part of the game. There are five forbidden films that can induce madness or release the Dark Gods that created them, speaking through the psychopathic director. Fiction. $14.99

Order today at www.happycloudpublishing.com!

www.ingramcontent.com/pod-product-compliance
Lightning Source LLC
Chambersburg PA
CBHW071301040426
42444CB00009B/1823